*The*

# NEW BELIEVER'S GUIDE

*to the*

# CHRISTIAN LIFE

## Books by Alex Early

*The New Believer's Guide to the Christian Life*

*The Reckless Love of God*

*The*

# NEW BELIEVER'S GUIDE

## to the

# CHRISTIAN LIFE

What Will Change, What Won't,
and Why It Matters

ALEX EARLY

**BETHANYHOUSE**
a division of Baker Publishing Group
Minneapolis, Minnesota

© 2016 by Alex Early

Published by Bethany House Publishers
11400 Hampshire Avenue South
Bloomington, Minnesota 55438
www.bethanyhouse.com

Bethany House Publishers is a division of
Baker Publishing Group, Grand Rapids, Michigan

Printed in the United States of America

Library of Congress Control Number: 2016938464

ISBN 978-0-7642-1836-1

Scripture quotations, unless otherwise noted, are from The Holy Bible, English Standard Version® (ESV®), copyright © 2001 by Crossway, a publishing ministry of Good News Publishers. Used by permission. All rights reserved. ESV Text Edition: 2011.

Scripture quotations marked NIV are from the Holy Bible, New International Version®. NIV®. Copyright © 1973, 1978, 1984, 2011 by Biblica, Inc.™ Used by permission of Zondervan. All rights reserved worldwide. www.zondervan.com.

Scripture quotations marked NASB are from the New American Standard Bible®, copyright © 1960, 1962, 1963, 1968, 1971, 1972, 1973, 1975, 1977, 1995 by The Lockman Foundation. Used by permission. www. Lockman.org

Scripture quotations marked NJB are from THE NEW JERUSALEM BIBLE, copyright © 1985 by Darton, Longman & Todd, Ltd. and Doubleday, a division of Random House, Inc. Reprinted by permission.

Scripture quotations marked NLT are from the Holy Bible, New Living Translation, copyright © 1996, 2004, 2015 by Tyndale House Foundation. Used by permission of Tyndale House Publishers, Inc., Carol Stream, Illinois 60188. All rights reserved.

Scripture quotations marked NKJV are from the New King James Version®. Copyright © 1982 by Thomas Nelson, Inc. Used by permission. All rights reserved.

Scripture quotation marked WE is taken from the Worldwide English New Testament.

All emphasis in Scripture, shown by italics, is the author's.

Cover design by Connie Gabbert

Author is represented by Wolgemuth and Associates.

16  17  18  19  20  21  22       7  6  5  4  3  2  1

I dedicate this book to my mother,

Bevy.

You have been and always will be my hero.
Your constant encouragement, steadfast love,
and Christlikeness are contagious.

I suppose the highest compliment comes from Jana,
as she has said for years, "If there's anyone I learn from
and want to be like in the whole world, it's your mom."
We love you so much! You're the best!

Turn around and believe that the good news that we are loved is better than we ever dared hope, and that to believe in that good news, to live out of it and toward it, to be in love with that good news, is of all glad things in this world the gladdest thing of all. Amen, and come, Lord Jesus.

—Frederick Buechner,
*The Clown in the Belfry:*
*Writings on Faith and Fiction*

# CONTENTS

# FOREWORD

In June of 1997 I became a Christian. It was one of those dramatic events that become legend—though they are certainly not the norm—but this isn't my book, so I won't get on that soapbox!

I was nearly sixteen. I'd grown up, to that point, identifying as a part-time Catholic. Though we had spent seasons (there's a great definition for this Christianese word in the appendix) in other church traditions, Catholicism was my foundation.

The period leading up to my salvation I now see with absolute clarity as organized and ordained by my heavenly Father, from start to finish. My dad's friend Johnny invited him to church, and my dad acquiesced because he was his friend and this new church seemed like a good idea for his two teenage boys. I'd describe my emotions around my first experience with this particular church as a mixture of fear, curiosity, and entertainment. The church was wildly, *wildly*, charismatic—white dress–wearing praise dancers, dramatic choir, and emotion-filled gospel presentations. They were weird to me then, but I'm certain Jesus was there.

11

We went with regularity, but I was only present, not engaged. My mother had become a Christian nearly eight years before this time in my life, after she'd attempted suicide and come to the end of herself in trying to solve some deep childhood trauma. Though I respected her decision, my thought was that she needed this church stuff to get better, and I'd be cool with it, but it wasn't for me. I was agnostic, though I had no term for it then.

Then something happened that I could not have anticipated: Jesus rescued my father from three generations of works-based, saved-by-being-a-good-man faith! He changed so dramatically that it almost seemed pretense to me. As I watched him, I noted the obvious genuineness of this new dad, and something softened in me. I can look back now and know that the Holy Spirit was preparing me for the moment I'd truly meet Jesus.

A few weeks after my father became a Christian, I was out playing basketball at a local park. A young man approached me whom I did not recognize, but apparently he recognized me. He came straight up to me and invited me to his youth group, which was not so coincidentally the youth group for the church we'd been attending. I said no. In fact, I'd say no four or five times. He just kept coming back, embarrassing me in front of my friends merely by his presence, and he kept inviting! I finally relented, only to get him to leave me alone. Little did I know that the day I relented would be the last day of my life that I didn't know the love of Jesus.

I look back on that time now and I have few regrets, but one stands out—after I became a Christian I wasn't completely sure what to do next. I am in no way saying that my local church wasn't trying to disciple me. I am, however, saying that often, even though many local churches have the very best intentions, new Christians can get lost in the shuffle. If not lost in the shuffle, shoved into leadership too quickly (i.e., I was leading a small group just weeks after becoming a Christian. I couldn't even find Deuteronomy in the Bible!)

I believe that's why Alex Early's work is so vital. As I began to read, my first thought was *Why hasn't anyone written this book before now?* As God would have it, my dear friend was the one for whom God was waiting.

Alex has taken great care to lovingly craft not just a "guide," but an insightful piece that answers many questions we don't even yet know we have when we're new to following Jesus. He covers many difficult topics with precision and love.

What do we do when we sin, once we've been forgiven of sin? How do we avoid spiraling into hopeless self-pity when we just can't seem to get it right? Does God expect us to always be "on"?

These few questions only scratch the surface of the depth and care that went into this book.

My early life in Christ was not "all roses," as Alex says. In fact, there was a real formula at work: Legalism + Sin = Condemnation. And it would repeat, for years. Only in my twenties did I really begin to understand grace and the gospel. I only share this because I truly believe that this book potentially would have altered the course of my early walk with Jesus.

I only say potentially because I am inherently rebellious, not because of any lack in this work. Yet, I have to believe that with a resource like this one, my first years would have been filled with exponentially less pain and more freedom. I pray that it will have the same promise for anyone starting out on the wondrous, complex, lifelong journey of following Jesus our King. Grace, and ever more grace to you!

Pastor Léonce B. Crump Jr.
founder, Renovation Church
author, *Renovate: Changing Who You Are by Loving Where You Are*

# INTRODUCTION

*I'm a Christian. Now What?*

You're a Christian! An amazing reality is now yours—you, my brother or sister, are a child of God! Welcome to the family! So why is a *New Believer's Guide* necessary? Because if you're a new believer in Jesus, you may feel like you're all alone in this process; but trust me, you're not. Here's what I mean: According to the International Bulletin of Missionary Research, there are, on average, 80,000 new Christians per day.[1] That's right. Not 8, not 80, not 800, but 80,000. That comes out to 56 every minute. Or 3,333 every hour, and 560,000 every week. That's approximately 2.43 million every month, 29.1 million every year. Right now, there are about 2 billion people on earth that are part of your new family—children of God. On top of this, since our faith is thousands of years old, countless others have understood and articulated this experience, though not everyone's experience is exactly the same, even those recorded in the Bible.

Like any book, this one cannot possibly exhaust all that goes into the Christian faith. The well is just that deep! However, the aim is to provide answers to common questions, give insights into regular routines and rhythms of the Christian life, and encourage you to grow in your discipleship with Jesus and in your relationships, both with those who also follow him and those who have yet to do so. We will cover things like identity, prayer, baptism, church membership, and giving—showing how these things profoundly impact your *real* life right here and right now as a disciple of Jesus.

The word *gospel* literally means "good news." The good news is that although you have sinned against God, he has loved, pursued, and forgiven you through Jesus. He has reconciled you to himself, and literally *nothing* in all of creation can separate you from this reality! Yes! Jesus lived the sinless life that we should have lived. Jesus died the sinner's death that we should have died. Jesus literally took our place and suffered the penalty for our sins, and not only that—the perfect, holy, blameless, righteous life he lived before God is now credited to our account! The Holy Spirit has drawn you to Jesus, granted you the ability to repent of your sins, and saved you completely and forever. This message of the radical, saving grace of God is called the gospel. To become a Christian is to become a follower of Jesus Christ—and not just on Sundays. Every hour of every day, we make it our aim to please him (Ephesians 2:10).

In some ways, this book functions like driving down the Interstate. At moments, there will be road signs indicating "what's coming up." At other times, we'll actually "exit the highway" and take time to explore some incredible things in God's Word, providing more information than you could get from a mere passing glance. What you won't find here are a lot of rules, checklists, and shortcuts to maturity. What you will find is that now that you're a child of God, by his grace, you are changed from the inside out, and that inward change of heart leads to an outward expression in daily life.

You have just had your life completely transformed by Jesus Christ. You might be thinking something like: *My life has been ransacked by Jesus! It seems like God has set a trap and got me! This feels almost like he had a plan!* And that is exactly what has happened. God had a plan from before time began to bring you into his family (Ephesians 1:4–5).

The Holy Spirit has regenerated you (Titus 3:5)—inwardly cleansed you and given you a new nature—called you and made you an entirely new creation (2 Corinthians 5:17). All of a sudden, you're probably realizing that your behavior is changing: your thoughts, attitudes, desires. You're seeing that you were created by God and for God (Romans 11:36; Ephesians 2:10). Yes, your existence on this earth is so much bigger than merely living for yourself, your career, your family, your friends, or your status. You are made for more than making money, being admired for your good looks, zoning out on endless vacations, and showing off all your newest toys. Keeping up with the Joneses really isn't what it's about anymore. In fact, it never was. As a Christian, you now know that you are actually created for the glory of God, and as one of his children ( John 1:12) your life is extremely significant (Romans 5:8).

## What Can You Expect?

What's your perception of what life with God is supposed to look like? Should you end up as a martyr in a place that is hostile to the message of Jesus? Is that "success"? Or, on the other hand, are you expecting a healthy, wealthy, beautiful, life with a belly full of good food and laughs with your innumerable friends? What will life with God be like? Or more important, what's it supposed to be like? Perhaps you've asked or thought about the following questions:

*Is Disneyland on the horizon? Or should I be anticipating torturous monotony in prayer, Bible study, and community projects, alongside the routine guilt-trip stewardship (money) talk from the pastor?*

*As a believer, can I count on mystical ecstasy day after day? What if I grow tired, weary, bored, despondent, confused, or annoyed with God along the way? Do I need to just plan on grinding my teeth in white-knuckled obedience to God? After all, Jesus bought me at an incredible price. How much do I owe him? Can he turn me in for a new model—someone that won't be so disappointing to him? Wait ... does he get disappointed with his people? Will he grow tired of me? How will I know if I've let him down? Is there a way I can make sure that I don't?*

These kinds of questions matter to new Christians. They also matter to those of us who've been in the faith for twenty years. I don't want to give you the impression that the Christian faith is a bed of roses. Nor do I want to give you the impression that you'll be thrown to the lions. I don't know my future, or your future for that matter.

What I do know is that in spite of the sufferings that we may endure along the way, God is good, loving, and in complete control. Jesus came to show us what a vibrant, abundant, deep-seated, soul-satisfying life looks like with God at the center of all that we are.

## Your Life . . . With God

The answer to the question "What will my life with God look like?" is pretty straightforward. Are you ready?

Your life with God is going to look like *your life* . . . but with God.

Yes, you are now changed, sealed, hidden with Christ in God, filled with the Holy Spirit, and one of his children. And yet, you're still in this world, trapped in your body, and your relationships (the good, the bad, and the ugly) haven't changed . . . yet.

But I imagine you've changed. You're thinking differently and feeling differently about a lot of things. Maybe you're seeing a little progress. Maybe you're seeing a lot of progress. So *you've* changed, yet a lot around you remains the same.

You may be thinking, *Okay. I'm in. What's next?*

## The Christian Life Isn't Easy

You may be under the impression, or illusion, that life will be all roses because you've repented of your sin and placed your faith in Jesus. Maybe you've already awakened to the fact: that simply isn't true.

There are those who teach that upon conversion you are entitled to a life of health, wealth, and great prosperity.

Suffering is for the sinners, and endless relaxation and delight are for the Christians. You will be surrounded by great friends who won't betray you (unlike Jesus' experience), you will have loads of money available to you all the time (unlike Jesus' experience), and you'll be healthy as a horse, until somehow you are miraculously raptured out of the earth at more than 100 years of age (unlike Jesus, to say the least). You're going to be the person that God calls on to get things done in the world. You'll be the diligent, unflinching, unwavering Christian who has an answer for everything, is afraid of nothing, and has the respect of everyone in your community.

If that's you, I take no pleasure in bursting your bubble (or maybe I do, just a little), but it must be done. Depending on your experience and how long you've been a Christian, you may already know where I'm going with this. You and I need to take an honest, sober look at the Bible, the Word of God, and talk about what it really means to be a Christian.

Jesus promised the disciples, "In this world you *will* have tribulation" (John 16:33). That was a fact for them, and it is for us to this day. As a Christian, you won't always have faith to walk on the water. You won't always believe, always love, always trust, always obey. Your prayers won't always be answered in the way you expect. You will have struggles in this life—with finances, relationships, your health.

Get this: You will even have significant doubts. In fact, in order for faith to be *faith*, you have to have some real doubts, real questions, and some real *mystery* at play. One of the greatest writers of our time, Frederick Buechner, says, "If you don't have any doubts, you are either kidding yourself or asleep.

Doubts are the ants in the pants of faith. They keep it alive and moving."[2] Having doubts doesn't get you thrown out of God's family. Rest assured, *God never—absolutely never—disowns his children.* God knew who you were before you met him, he knows your current struggles and future failures, and he has covenanted to walk with you anyway, no matter what.

The early Christians weren't known for their pickets and protests. Their reputation wasn't earned by having a neat and tidy theological answer for every single nuance pertaining to God, faith, and the world. They didn't know it all, but they did know God. The saints of the first century weren't known for their T-shirts, bumper stickers, coffee cups, and pat clichés. That's not to say they didn't make bold stands—they most certainly did, as many were killed because of their faith. Moreover, their theology—by the looks of church history— was deep and wide. They knew *what* they believed and *why* they believed it. Their theology expressed itself in ways that "turned the world upside down" (Acts 17:6). This is because their theology wasn't mere cold, scientific, impersonal propositions. No! Their theology set their hearts ablaze, and it was demonstrated in their words, their deeds, and their servant-driven, sacrificial, joyous, infectious, contagious love.

Six times in the book of Acts, the early Christians were referred to as "followers of the Way" (Acts 9:2; 19:9, 23; 22:4; 24:14, 22). In all likelihood, this name was derived from Jesus' declaration that he is "the way, and the truth, and the life" ( John 14:6). In short, Christians are not only "on their way," they're following *the Way*; they're following *Jesus.* Though imperfect, as seen throughout the letters in the New Testament, they were striving to love one another just as Jesus instructed them to do. In fact, their reputation was unlike anything the world had ever seen. They'd heard the gospel. They'd received grace. They knew Jesus. There is much to be said about the early followers of Jesus, but just look at this excerpt, written in AD 130, by an unknown author, to see what early Christians were known for:

> They dwell in their own countries, but simply as sojourners. As citizens, they share in all things with others and yet endure all things as if foreigners. Every foreign land is to them as their native country, and every land of their birth as a land of strangers. They marry, as do all [others]; they beget children; but they do not destroy their offspring. They have a common table, but not a common bed. They are in the flesh, but they do not live after the flesh. They pass their days on earth but they are citizens of heaven. They obey the prescribed laws, and at the same time surpass the laws by their lives. They love all men, and are persecuted by all. They are unknown and condemned; they are put to death, and restored to life. They are poor, yet make many rich; they are in lack of all things, and yet abound in all; they are dishonored, and yet in their very dishonor are glorified. They are evil spoken of, and yet are justified; they are reviled, and bless; they are insulted, and repay the insult with honor; they do good, yet are punished as evildoers.[3]

Brothers and sisters, that's your family. And that's what you can expect the Christian life to be like. What makes all of this sacrifice, selflessness, honor, and love possible or even worth it? They, like you, found what Jesus described as "the treasure."

In one parable, two small sentences, Jesus lets us in on what's behind all of this sacrifice: "The kingdom of heaven is like treasure hidden in a field, which a man found and covered up. Then in his joy he goes and sells all that he has and buys that field" (Matthew 13:44).

Entering the kingdom is done with joy! And this joy is not intended to be found only when thinking about your conversion. This joy is intended to accompany the rest of your life! The challenges of discipleship are accompanied by a deeper, greater, abiding *joy*.

## The Direction of the Book

This book does not offer practical steps on how to join a small-group Bible study, be the savvy Christian evangelist on the block, have daily prayer and Bible reading, or serve your community. All of those things are essential to a growing faith. But those are simply a few of the "whats" of discipleship. I want to talk about the "whys" that drive those disciplines. This is aimed at our hearts. Our motives matter big time. What drives our Christian obedience, sacrifice, and service is not the ulterior motive of getting God's love. It is the fact that we already are the beloved of God that motivates us to do what we do.

One of the early themes of this book is the simple fact that life with God is not always fun. Abundant? Yes. Fun? Not necessarily.

We will focus on living our lives in the light of Jesus' sacrifice, dying to sin, and finding life in obeying Jesus' commandments.

We will talk about your identity being grounded not in what you do (or don't do) in this world, but in who Jesus is and what he's done for you.

I also want to challenge you to exchange your contractual relationship with God for what he offers instead—namely, a covenant. What does this mean? In a nutshell, God wants to know you rather than just use you, and this profoundly impacts the way you go about living your life with him.

If you are going to experience the depths of knowing God, it's going to require an incredible amount of transparency, brokenness, and vulnerability with a God who loves you and made you for himself. That's what prayer is all about.

From there I want to talk about how men and women in the Bible all struggled when it came to obedience. The reality is that God himself does in fact make tall orders and big requests of his people. Since you are one of those people, you should expect the same.

We'll also get into what baptism is and why we do it.

Then I'll address the meaning and importance of becoming a member of a local church. Yet membership isn't all there is to this thing called church. We'll also discuss the incredible gift of being a part of and practicing gospel-centered community.

We will take a little space to talk about a big topic—money. The Bible speaks a lot about the money we have and how we're to steward it as the children of God.

We'll conclude by pressing every believer toward real maturity in the faith.

The appendix of the book is a glossary that defines about thirty "Christianese" terms. These are expressions you'll hear around the church.

One final thing to mention: At the end of each chapter I've included a few questions for you to consider as you reflect on what you've read.

# WE WORK *FROM* NOT *FOR* OUR IDENTITY

> Modern people have things completely back
> to front: Professing to be unsure of God, they
> pretend to be sure of themselves. Followers
> of Christ put things the other way around:
> Unsure of ourselves, we are sure of God.
>
> —Os Guinness, *The Call*

The entire message of the Bible is one of grace, hope, forgiveness, and love—all unearned, ill-deserved, and completely without condition! The love of God is reckless, pervasive, and unstoppable. The love of God knows no limits or boundaries! Thus far, though billions have tried, none have been able to stop the work of God.

The love of God is not reserved for only the rich or only the poor. It is not only for straight people, Republicans, or humanitarians. The love of God cannot be confined within the walls of a local church building. The love of God is not rhetoric or wishful thinking. It cannot be shrunk down to a coffee cup or bumper sticker or cliché. The love of God does not fall asleep at the wheel, but is always alive, brilliant, and blazing! God's love is not just for the world out there, not just for the church down the street, not just for the pastor or missionary, but for you in that chair right there, right now, with all your past mistakes, all your present skepticism, and all the stubborn "so what's?" and "prove it to me's" that may be going on in your head right now. Yes, it is for *you*.

In fact, being a new Christian, you've come to terms with or are at least beginning to come to terms with the fact that God hasn't insisted on your getting better or trying harder in order to get into his family. If you come with empty hands, you come with all you need. God's love isn't fickle, moody, or affordable. It is something that must be given to you, and the only thing more offensive to God than your sin is your feeble attempt to *earn* his loving affection. It is *free.* God is *for* us.

## Questions Arise

Now, with all of this grace talk, questions start to arise . . . don't they? For example, you might be thinking, *Alex, you're saying God loves me on my worst day. So . . . is sin okay? Or does sin not bother God anymore once we're in Christ?*

Those are legitimate questions in light of such scandalous grace. Paul asks, "What shall we say then? Are we to continue in sin that grace may abound?" (Romans 6:1). The reasoning goes, "If I sin a lot and I get more grace, then shouldn't I just keep sinning so that I can get more grace?" That is certainly not at all what the Bible teaches. Paul responds to his own question by saying, "By no means!" (v. 2).

## Live at the Foot of the Cross

You see, this way of thinking, and living, is not just sloppy theology and discipleship. It is complete rebellion against God! If you find yourself facing temptation to sin, and you flippantly say, "So what? Grace will cover this" or "I can just charge this sin to Jesus' account," you should have no confidence that you have actually experienced the grace of God in the first place. Grace changes our appetites. What we used to love, we no longer crave. The things we used to despise, we now desire. Our diet changes because our appetite changes. As a true Christian, we should actually long for God, his will, his Word, his work in our lives, and not our own.

This is why we must live our lives at the foot of the cross. By this, I mean that we meditate on the meaning of Jesus' death and we live grateful, joyful, holy lives. It is at the cross of Jesus that we get our clearest instructions on love and discipleship. It's hard to live at the foot of the cross, knowing who died for you there, bearing all your sin, your guilt, and your shame, and then treat his sacrifice as common or trivial.

Maybe you've met some folks who say they know God, but in spite of their claim, they're rude, grouchy, unkind, and overloaded with worry, stress, and anxiety. Words like *contentment, hope,* and *peace* don't come to mind when you think of them. Based on these people, you might think God couldn't care less about your joy. And yet that is precisely what he's after! Jesus said he wants his disciples to remain close to him so that "your joy may be full" (John 15:11). Personally speaking, I grew up in a Christian home and have known Jesus for twenty years, and I've never seen a single Christian who seeks to live their life at the foot of the cross of Jesus and treats sin lightly or has an empty joy-tank.

## The Prodigal Son:
## What Do You Think Grace Did to Him?

Consider the famous parable of the prodigal son in Luke 15. The younger of two sons asked for his inheritance and squandered it all away on reckless living. He ended up broke, face-down in the mud, with nowhere to go. But then "he came to his senses" (v.17 NIV) and went back to his father in the hope of being brought on to work as a hired hand. And yet, to his surprise, he was joyously received back by his father, who threw an extravagant party because they had been reunited.

Do you think the son, once he found out how gracious and welcoming his father was, really wanted to go back to the prostitutes and partying? Did he really think to himself, *My dad is such a sucker. He lets me get away with anything. I'll break his heart a hundred times over. Who cares? I'm going to do it my way.* Hardly. The following morning, waking up at his father's home was an overwhelming picture of grace. He must've thought to himself, *I certainly don't belong here. And yet I belong here with my father. I don't want to please my father in order to get grace, but rather because I've received grace, I want to please my father.*

## Dying to Sin

Look closely at what Paul says in Romans 6:2: "How can we who died to sin still live in it?" He does not say, "Sin dies to the believer." Oh no! Paul tells us that the *believer* dies to sin. These are radically different. This explains the tension, the struggle between following Jesus and the fact that sin is still tempting to us.

Scholar Robert Mounce says, "Christ's death *for* sin becomes our death *to* sin."[1] Again, you and I are not called to behavior modification, a moral tweak here and there. You and I are called to die to sin and live to Christ. The Puritan preacher John Owen said, "Be killing sin or sin will be killing you."[2] This is a long, ongoing process of becoming more like Jesus . . . it's called sanctification.

> Do you not know that all of us who have been baptized into Christ Jesus were baptized into his death? We were buried therefore with him by baptism into death, in order that, just as Christ was raised from the dead by the glory of the Father, we too might walk in newness of life. For if we have been united with him in a death like his, we shall certainly be united with him in a resurrection like his. We know that our old self was crucified with him in order that the body of sin might be brought to nothing, so that we would no longer be enslaved to sin. For one who has died has been set free from sin. Now if we have died with Christ, we believe that we will also live with him. We know that Christ, being raised from the dead, will never die again; death no longer has dominion over him. For the death he died he died to sin, once for all, but the life he lives he lives to God. So you also must consider yourselves dead to sin and alive to God in Christ Jesus.

Let not sin therefore reign in your mortal body, to make you obey its passions. Do not present your members to sin as instruments for unrighteousness, but present yourselves to God as those who have been brought from death to life, and your members to God as instruments for righteousness. For sin will have no dominion over you, since you are not under law but under grace.

Romans 6:3–14

## "Die to Sin"—What? How?

Jesus died for our sins, and through the Holy Spirit we are enabled to walk in joyous obedience to God. This is amazing grace! You may be under the impression that Christianity is a doom and gloom religion, and perhaps that's why for quite some time you didn't want to become a Christian. Maybe your understanding was one-sided—"You have to die to sin." And if that were the message, there's no way we could call it good news! That's because it isn't in our nature to die to sin. To turn down temptation does not feel humanly possible. Yet we are empowered by the Holy Spirit to live our lives following Jesus *and* dying to sin. The Greek expression translated "newness of life" (Romans 6:4) is better rendered "a new sphere, which is life."[3] You've been adopted into a new family, brought into an entirely new world.

Baptism here (v. 3) is not referring to your water baptism, but is shorthand for your conversion experience as a whole. Paul says you are "no longer . . . enslaved to sin" (v. 6). As a Christian, you'll need to know this and cling to this all the way through to your deathbed. Will you still sin sometimes?

Yes. However, if you're a Christian, you will genuinely repent and move along. When you sin, it no longer feels right. You're no longer a slave to it. You're free.

I once heard a vivid description of a Christian having fellowship with sin and death. A sinning Christian can be likened to one digging up a corpse and bringing it to the dinner table, pretending to have a conversation with it. That is gross, revolting, and completely insane! Because the living have no fellowship with the dead.

## Your Self-Perception

Here's how you need to think about yourself, consider yourself, see yourself, meditate on your identity as a child of God: "Dead to sin and alive to God" (Romans 6:11). Paul is telling you how to think. Your flesh is no longer allowed to tell you who you are. But you can't do this apart from the Holy Spirit. If you try to consider yourself dead to sin apart from the saving work of Christ and the indwelling Holy Spirit, you will be miserable. Because to live as God would have you live requires that God be living through you. Legalism is man's attempt at sanctification apart from the justifying work of Jesus and the indwelling, empowering, ongoing presence of the Holy Spirit.

Paul tells us, "Do not present your members to sin as instruments of unrighteousness, but present yourselves to God as those who have been brought from death to life, and your members to God as instruments for righteousness" (Romans 6:13). You and I are faced with a presentation of our bodies to one of two places. The question is not "Will I present my body to God or to sin?" The question is "To whom will I present my body?" Many Christians think of their spiritual lives as divorced from their physical bodies—that their Christian life is to be private, and their spirituality is something "out there in the heavens" or "in my heart" or "in my head" or some sort of existential way of thinking. But this kind of thinking comes from Plato, not God.

Plato was a famous Greek philosopher who taught that the body is bad and the spirit is good. This carried over into the way many Christians see themselves. However, the Bible doesn't present us with this dualistic way of thinking. Rather, you are a soul that has a body wrapped around it. Therefore, what you do physically is a window into who or what your soul values.

## Obey! Obey! Obey!

Paul tells us, "By grace you have been saved through faith. And this is not your own doing; it is the gift of God, not a result of works, so that no one may boast. For we are his workmanship, created in Christ Jesus for good works, which God prepared beforehand, that we should walk in them" (Ephesians 2:8–10).

It is critical that we keep constantly before our eyes the reality that we are saved by the grace of God and not by any works of our own. The good works that follow and flow from our salvation are not what justify us before God. We're justified by Christ and saved by grace. The good works are evidence of the ongoing, inward reality that we are in a relationship with the living God. Thus, Paul admonishes us to "work out your salvation with fear and trembling, for it is God who works in you, both to will and to work for his good pleasure" (Philippians 2:12–13). Catch that! We work *out* what God works *in* us. We don't work *at,* work *for,* or work *toward* our salvation! We are called to work *out* our salvation. Paul is not saying that we are free of all divine commands!

Jesus commands us to love our neighbor (Luke 10:36–37). Jesus commands us to forsake sin (Matthew 18:6), to walk in holiness (5:27–30). Jesus commands us to go into the world and make disciples (28:18–20). Paul emphasizes the fact that the grace that saves us is the same grace that transforms us, and thus we are met with the incredible challenge and distinct privilege of working out all that God has worked into our hearts:

> What then? Are we to sin because we are not under law but under grace? By no means! Do you not know that if you present yourselves to anyone as obedient slaves, you are slaves of the one whom you obey, either of sin, which leads to death, or of obedience, which leads to righteousness? But thanks be to God, that you who were once slaves of sin have become obedient from the heart to the standard of teaching to which you were committed, and, having been set free from sin, have become slaves of righteousness. I am speaking in human terms, because of your natural limitations. For just as you once presented your members as slaves to impurity and to lawlessness leading to more lawlessness, so now present your members as slaves to righteousness leading to sanctification.

For when you were slaves of sin, you were free in regard to righteousness. But what fruit were you getting at that time from the things of which you are now ashamed? For the end of those things is death. But now that you have been set free from sin and have become slaves of God, the fruit you get leads to sanctification and its end, eternal life. For the wages of sin is death, but the free gift of God is eternal life in Christ Jesus our Lord.

Romans 6:15–23

Why go back and look at this relationship we have with sin and grace? Because sin is deceitful (Hebrews 3:13), and we may be tempted to accept the sin in our lives instead of fighting against it, or we may think that because we sin God will kick us out of the family.

Now Paul picks up the question again concerning the relationship of sin and grace: *"Well then, if I'm not under the law anymore, who cares if I sin?"* the logic goes. The allurement will come throughout your life as a Christian to go lightly on sin and take the grace of God for granted. But as children of God, we do not take lightly what Jesus died to separate us from. Paul calls us back to our identity—being slaves of righteousness. The issue ever set before you for the rest of your life is not *if* you will be a slave. The question is "Whose slave will you be?" A slave of sin or a slave of righteousness—these are our only options. There's no commonality, no friendship between these two slave masters. They absolutely will not share you with each other. God will not share you with sin. And sin will not share you with God. You will be wholly devoted to one or the other.

## The Hour I First Believed

In this section of Romans, Paul says, "But what fruit were you getting at that time from the things of which you are now ashamed? For the end of those things is death" (v. 21). He is helping us recall what life was like when we lived without God. He asks, "How did that work out for you?" He's pushing us to go back and reflect on the time when we did not know Jesus. I'm telling you, if you want to see your faith catch fire, think back to where you were, who you were with, what you were up to in the days just before you met Jesus. "For the end of those things is death," meaning you could taste death on every breath.

A few years ago, I was in Seattle, taking a walk with my good friend Nathan Burke. We were walking along the waterfront, looking at the fantastic houseboats painted in some of the most extravagant colors. As we passed beneath the Fremont Bridge, Nate said, "You know that line in 'Amazing Grace' that says, 'How precious did that grace appear the hour I first believed'?"

"Of course, I do, man. Why?" I replied.

He said, "I have to go back to that moment in time a lot and remember what that first hour was like."

I've thought about that a lot since our conversation. The apostle Paul talks about his past—not in a shaming, condemning way, but neither does he glorify his past before meeting Jesus. Essentially, Paul never forgot where he came from. He remembered his hour of amazing grace, and it served to ground him further in Jesus and the gospel.

You may not be able to say, "This is the exact moment, the exact place I was standing, when Jesus became my Savior and Lord." But you will probably be able to say, "Around this time in my life (around this *hour*), Jesus changed my life." I want to encourage you never to forget that hour, to keep it ever before you. I've found that when I'm feeling lazy or burned out in my Christian faith, few things sober me up and reorient me to following Jesus and pursuing him like remembering where I was the night before he gloriously saved me.

All of your sin, all of your selfishness, all of your rebellion—ends in death. Your sin earned you the just wrath of God. And Paul is exclaiming that not one drop of justice is ever coming to you! *Never.* You are now a child of God, a slave of righteousness, and you are secure in his love.

## Condemnation vs. Conviction

Another question: "What am I feeling, or rather what am I *supposed* to feel when I sin *after* becoming a Christian?" Yes, *every* Christian sins. *Every* Christian struggles and must daily take up his or her cross (Matthew 16:24) and die to sin (1 Corinthians 15:31). There is coming a day in which this will no longer be the case, because you and I, alongside every other believer, will be what Paul describes as "glorified" (Romans 8:30).

Essentially, you will have one of two experiences upon rebelling against God. You must learn to discern between the two: condemnation and conviction. They may sound the same, but they are worlds apart, much like seeing two stars at night that look so close they appear to be one. Yet through a telescope, you see that they are miles apart.

Condemnation can come from your flesh, the devil, your critics, or even your own conscience. Condemnation is always punitive and never restorative. Condemnation compounds the fracture and makes a bad situation worse. Condemnation is painful, destructive, and crippling to a Christian. We must remember that Jesus did not come to judge or condemn the world, including you (John 3:17; 8:11). As one of God's children, you received a new wardrobe, and condemnation was not included because it no longer fits.

Conviction is entirely different. Conviction comes from the Holy Spirit. Jesus said the Holy Spirit "will convict the world concerning sin and righteousness and judgment" (John 16:8). Conviction is always helpful and constructive, and comes with the aim of being restorative. Conviction is the result of God's kindness that leads to repentance (Romans 2:4). Conviction from the Holy Spirit enables us to "walk in the light, as he is in the light" (1 John 1:7). Conviction is not God nitpicking your life. Conviction is not God's attempt to ground you down to a depressed mound of powder. Conviction is God's reminder that he has something better for you.

What is the way out from under condemnation? How can you be sure that you are under conviction instead, which leads to growth in your life with God? Meditate on the cross of Jesus. Go to that most condemned place and person in history and see your sin being judged. Your sin was not swept under the rug. It was not treated lightly. It was not ignored. Your sin was nailed to the cross of Jesus (Colossians 2:14). It is at the cross that we see how much God hates sin. It is there that we see the depth of his love that drove him to die in order to be with us forever.

St. Francis de Sales once said, "It is upon Calvary of Christ's cross that the saints meditate, contemplate, and come to experience their Lord."[4]

*The Book of Common Prayer* teaches us to pray:

> Most merciful God,
> we confess that we have sinned against you
> in thought, word, and deed,
> by what we have done,
> and by what we have left undone.
> We have not loved you with our whole heart;
> we have not loved our neighbors as ourselves.
> We are truly sorry and we humbly repent.
> For the sake of your Son Jesus Christ,
> have mercy on us and forgive us;
> that we may delight in your will
> and walk in your ways,
> to the glory of your Name. Amen.[5]

Brothers and sisters, welcome to the family.

God loves the sinner, not because He is drawn to him by his lovableness, but because, in spite of man's unloveliness, God sets His mind and will on seeking man's highest good. This is what is amazing about God's love.[6]

## Not Good Advice

This radical gospel dramatically reorients us. I want you to capture the immensity with which the apostle Paul speaks. He does not talk about the Christian life as a trivial change of mind, or the gospel as a bit of data that persuades you to think differently or revamp your ethics a tad. That's not even close! He speaks about being dead or alive (Ephesians

2:1–5). There is no in-between state in his mind. You are dead in sin or alive in Christ.

Theologian Michael Horton says it well:

> Reduce Christianity to good advice and it blends in perfectly with the culture of *life coaching*. It might seem relevant, but it is actually lost in the marketplace of moralistic therapies. When we pitch Christianity as the best method of personal improvement, complete with testimonies about how much better we are ever since we "surrendered all," non-Christians can legitimately demand of us, "What right do you have to say that yours is the only source of happiness, meaning, exciting experiences, and moral betterment?" Jesus is clearly not the only effective way to a better life or to being a better me. One can lose weight, stop smoking, improve one's marriage, and become a nicer person without Jesus.[7]

What you receive from Jesus is not just a different version of you or a better version of you. It is not a you that has a bit more potential. No! It is a totally new you! You are a new creation through being "in Christ" right now, not later. That's the radical scandal of the gospel! You don't have an identity to earn or strive for. It is something freely given to you by God! We'll explore this identity in the next chapter.

## QUESTIONS TO CONSIDER

1. What does it mean to you to know that your identity is not something that is achieved but rather something received?

2. Think about the difference between conviction and condemnation. How can you tell which one you're experiencing?

3. Why do you think that the temptation to abuse God's grace is so strong?

4. Think about the hour you first believed. What was that like?

**2**

# You Are a Beloved Child of God

It is better to be a child of God than king of
the whole world.

—Saint Aloysius Gonzaga

As a Christian, you're probably discovering that so much
is changing about you. You're realizing that you no longer
need to be intimidated (Proverbs 29:25). You are no longer
made up of your wins or your losses, your successes or failures, your best day or worst day. Your identity is completely
founded in Jesus Christ—his perfect life, his sacrificial death,
and his resurrection from the dead (Romans 3:23; 6:23;
2 Corinthians 5:21). You are new. You've been given a new
identity.

## A Brand-New Identity

That word *identity* really does something to us as modern people, doesn't it? Answering the question "Who am I?" isn't so easy. In an age where we create our online profiles, we're tempted to merely show the highlights of our lives. The food we eat, the places we go, the people we're with, the experiences we're having—the tasty, the fun, the exciting, the interesting. Yes, the version of you that you wish were true twenty-four hours a day, seven days a week is what you and I post online for people to "like" and wish they could "share" in with us.

Ever since Genesis 3, when sin entered the world, our fundamental identity has been lost, and we've been in a constant search to recover it. Now it just seems that we've found more and more ways to further posture ourselves and use work, or one another, or technology to serve as a proverbial fig leaf to hide our nakedness. There was a day when the king was the celebrity of the land. But now, with our cameras, status updates, and filters to make ourselves, our friends, and our experiences look all the better, we are provided with a little taste of what it must feel like to be king for a day. Yet identity is received, not achieved.

Social media aside, we are tempted to derive our identity from our work, our relationships, our status, our education, or anything else that is easily quantifiable, able to be judged and categorized. So when I mention the fact that your *identity* has changed through becoming a Christian, it really does strike a nerve, sounding completely crazy and even scary to almost anyone. Everything is now dramatically affected by this all-consuming relationship that you have entered into with God. This is because God engages all of you, not just part of you.

My friend Krish Kandiah describes the Christian life as a *paradox*. You are no longer completely liberal or completely conservative. You fit in, and at the same time you don't. As the Bible puts it, you are in the world but not of the world (John 15:19; Romans 12:2), and this world is not your home because you're really just a sojourner on your way to where your true citizenship lies, in heaven (Psalm 119:19; Philippians 3:20; 1 Peter 2:11).

Furthermore, as a child of God, you don't have to reject everything in creation and culture. But at the same time you don't have to agree with everything that goes on in the world, either. In this world you will have times when you're comfortable, and at the same time you live in a place where Jesus said you would be hated (Matthew 10:22; John 15:18). Because of the gospel, we are not the sum of our work life, relationship status, accomplishments, and failures. Because of what, or rather who, is available to us in the gospel, as Christians, we understand that all of our identity comes from him. So let's take a moment to walk through our identity as the children of God.

## Who Am I?

There are some questions that we ask only once in life and the answer satisfies us, never to be challenged again. For example, $2 + 2 = 4$. A hot stove will burn your hand if you touch it. *Star Wars* is infinitely better than *Star Trek*, and so on. Then there are other questions that arise again and again throughout our lives. They're the deep questions, the existential questions, the questions of meaning, purpose, and identity. Questions like "Who am I?" "Why am I here?" "Where do I belong?" The need to know exactly *who* we are, *where* we come from, and where we are *going* seems to intensify as we get older. Unexpected tragedies and major life transitions cause us to soberly assess the really big stuff that not only makes up our worldview but also contributes a considerable amount to how we understand ourselves.

In an ever-changing, unpredictable world, is it possible to really know who we are? Today we are constantly bombarded by our culture and social media with millions of answers to our questions: *"This is who you are!" "No! This is who you are!" "Wear this!" "Eat that!" "Go here!" "Think this way!" "Vote for him!" "Go to that school!" "Believe this!" "Reject that!"* Just going to the grocery store can seem a bit overwhelming. A few years ago, Barry Schwartz, who serves as professor of Social Theory and Social Action at Swarthmore College in Pennsylvania, wrote a book entitled *The Paradox of Choice.* Pastor Kevin DeYoung captured the big idea nicely as he gives a glimpse into what Dr. Schwartz is getting at:

> He found 285 varieties of cookies, 13 sports drinks, 65 box drinks, 85 kids' juices, 75 iced teas, 95 types of chips and pretzels, 15 kinds of bottled water, 80 different pain relievers, 40 options for toothpaste, 150 lipsticks, 360 types of shampoo, 90 different cold remedies, 230 soups, 75 instant gravies, 275 varieties of cereal, 64 types of barbeque sauce, and 22 types of frozen waffles.[1]

And on and on it goes. Just like a clown's endless rainbow-colored Kleenex that keeps flowing out of the box, so it is with the smorgasbord of options available to us today. We're tempted to think: *I am who I am sleeping with; I am my kid's performance on the soccer field;* or *I am exactly how much I make.* This is an absolutely taxing and draining experience. It fills us with anxiety, uncertainty, and deep frustration. Even on our best day, we're tempted to wonder things like *Did I marry the right person? Did I major in the right subject? Do I have the right job? Am I living in the right place?* One person will affirm me, validate me, and tell me I made it. The next will critique me, criticize me, and tell me I blew it. This guy says I am to be purpose-driven and that guy tells me there's no purpose to the world. Is there a rock I can stand on, a place I can go that will calm all the swirling questions in my head? As a Christian, you know that answer is *yes!* And you answer yes not in some shrouded, look-professional false assurance, but in the deep confidence a child has in his parent.

You've been given the invaluable gift of experiencing peace with God, yourself, and others. You belong to God not as a piece of creation in general, but as a *beloved* child. The ongoing temptations and endless questions of identity and purpose don't have to shake you. You, like every other believer throughout the great history of our faith, have committed yourself to the timeless truths of Scripture and understand that regardless of what comes your way, your identity is *secure* in Jesus.

The core of a Christian is not defined by what she does, but rather who she *is* in Christ. That is, the identity of every Christian is not something that is earned or achieved. Instead, the believer *receives* her identity from God the Father, grounds herself in the person and work of Jesus, and lives through the indwelling and empowering of the Holy Spirit.

It is imperative to understand this early on in the faith and to repeat it throughout one's entire life: Christian identity is not found in how many dollars you give, church meetings you attend, mission trips you go on, churches you plant, prayers you pray, Scriptures you memorize, degrees you earn, or bumper stickers you plaster on the back of your car. To have been sought, bought, and kept by Jesus is literally *all* there is to your identity. Jesus has settled your past, dwells with you in the present, and is guaranteed to be yours for the never-ending future. And it is from *this* identity that all the disciplines of the faith like prayer, fasting, giving, etc., fall into place because the heart has been regenerated, the mind has been renewed, and the soul has found its resting place. Your identity is secure as a beloved child of God.

## Who You Are: A Child of God

Please don't dismiss this section as childish or elementary. Those of us who belong to the covenant of God have plenty of metaphors to draw from in Scripture that speak to our identity, such as sheep, workmen, soldiers, and so on. But the relational dynamic goes through the roof as the apostles begin to refer to us as the *"children of God."*

If you've ever had a course in anthropology, you've come across the discussion about whether or not human identity is received or achieved or a mix of both. In the gospel, it is completely one-sided; your identity is totally *received* through faith. In Galatians 3:26, Paul says, "For in Christ Jesus you are all sons of God, through faith." In fact, your identity was settled long before you were born, even before the foundations of the world were laid. In Ephesians 1:4–6, we read, "He chose us in him before the creation of the world to be holy and blameless in his sight. In love he predestined us for adoption to sonship through Jesus Christ, in accordance with his pleasure and will—to the praise of his glorious grace, which he has freely given us in the One he loves" (NIV).

I know the word *predestination* is a hot button for many. In fact, debates over the sovereign will of God and the free will of man have raged for centuries and will continue until the end of time. Let me admonish you, before you get hung up on the nuances of what is meant by *predestination,* to slow down and catch that four-letter word Paul used: *love.* It was *in love* that God saved you. It was *in love* that he made you his son or his daughter. It was *in love* that God created you and gave you faith, repentance, forgiveness, salvation, the kingdom, his covenants, his promises, his Word, his Spirit, his very *self.* If there's anything to get hung up on in these verses, it is the incredible love of God.

## Getting Your Childhood Back

When Jesus taught about the kingdom of God, he did so in a way that was nothing less than revolutionary. The way he lived, loved, led, and taught shattered all of our conceptions of the nature and character of God. It turns out God is more holy and more loving than any of us could ever have dreamed. During his ministry here on earth, Jesus drew the boldest lines in the sand this world has ever known. Then, as now, the "sophisticated" scoffed at Jesus' constant attention to the no-names, the not-good-enough, the poor, the easily overlooked, the so-called insignificant people that fill this world. When it came to talking about how God relates to those with whom he is reconciled, he spoke of children, not employees.

On at least one occasion, Jesus said, "Unless you turn and become like children, you will never enter the kingdom of heaven" (Matthew 18:3). What on earth could he be talking about? What does he mean by this? Consider that many believe the way into the kingdom is through violence, or education, or one's own moral goodness. You've got to earn your way in because, after all, there's no such thing as a free lunch. But Jesus is the King of giving out free lunches. Jesus teaches that the only way to grow up is to grow down. The only way to go forward is to go backward. The only way to save your soul is to lose it in his grace. Jesus never referred to his disciples as the strong, informed, and accomplished. Rather, when speaking to grown men, who previously ran fishing businesses or collected taxes, he addressed them as "children." I wonder if they ever got used to that. I wonder if you will.

Jesus' referring to his disciples as children is certainly curious. Today, this may not be too hard for many of us to come to terms with because we tend to adore children (though certainly not all do). We take hundreds of pictures of our kids, spend insane amounts of money taking them to Disneyland

and other adventures, and on Daddy dates. We often envy them in small ways because they don't have much to worry about compared to our going to work, paying the rent, and trying to keep afloat.

But in Jesus' day, children weren't praised or prized. There were no "My child is an all-star at Jerusalem Elementary School" stickers on the back of their camels. Rather, children were to be seen and not heard. Many considered children to be just another mouth to feed, a responsibility to fulfill. But Jesus pressed beyond this way of seeing children as a burden and rather delighted in them as a blessing. Jesus was more interested in the childlike trust, curiosity, and wonder that fills a preschooler's eyes on Christmas morning or in the park swing on a Sunday afternoon.

As we grow older, the wonder, the trust, the childlikeness within us begins to shrivel due to pain, circumstances, or the overall busyness of life. Maybe you're like me, and you often daydream of playing in the creek in the backyard with your little brother, or wanting to feel that existential bliss of getting snowed in on a school day. Or how about when the ice cream truck came to your neighborhood on a summer day and there was just enough loose change in the junk drawer in the kitchen to take an afternoon from good to great? *Childhood.*

Some of you reading this lost your childhood because of something someone did to you, robbing you of your innocence. Maybe thinking of your childhood is hard because times were tough for one reason or another. And while the gospel doesn't change what happened in the past, one of the greatest gifts God gives us is a second childhood, a truer childhood, an authentic childhood that lasts for a lifetime and beyond.

The Bible teaches us to refer to God our Father as "Abba," a close, dear, tender name used only by those who burn with great affection for him. Our Abba longs, yearns, and even quakes for his children, you and I, to become our truest selves in him. We're at our most authentic not when we're scourging ourselves for our failures or jockeying for positions, but when we're basking in his love, trusting him with all our hearts, and bringing him our prayers—wilted dandelions, which he happily receives. Do you think this is sloppy sentimentalism? It isn't. The good news of a gracious God who gave his Son to die in our place for our vile sins turns hearts of stone to hearts of flesh.

Jesus, the very Son of God, our Big Brother, brought us into the family of God. This reality moved all of the disciples, but it seems to have gripped John in an utterly profound way as he mentions followers of Jesus being "children of God" five times in his writings. In 1 John 3:1, he writes to the church, "See what kind of love the Father has given to us, that we should be called children of God; and so we are." To be a child of God is no small thing, for it is the Almighty, eternal, omnipresent, omnipotent King of Kings and Lord of Lords who is our tender Abba Father! Maybe you've never considered this for more than thirty seconds, but I strongly encourage you to make it a habit to remind yourself that you are a child of God! So before proceeding, would you consider praying with me?

*Abba, I know I don't deserve to be one of your blessed children in whom you delight, but I am. Jesus was and is your Son. But to call me your child is to leave me nearly speechless. I have sinned in more ways than I can count, and you've forgiven me for everything done or left undone. The temptation to believe the lie that you'd rather I be your employee than your child is huge. I'm prone toward posturing and positioning myself in an attempt to earn your love. Place your heart in mine and hide mine in yours. Help me understand just how affectionate you are toward me. Please keep me grounded in this nearly unfathomable reality. Abba, I am your child. Abba, I belong to you.*

## Foreign Love

John was absolutely astonished that he would be referred to as one of God's children. Originally, speaking of "what kind" of love (1 John 3:1) the Father has given us meant "of what country." John Stott says, "The Father's love is so unearthly, so foreign to this world, that [John] wonders from what country it may come."[2]

If you've ever traveled internationally, the weight of this verse will really sink in here. I've traveled a good bit internationally and have gotten used to the chaos that accompanies such an endeavor. However, the first time I had no idea all that I'd experience. At nineteen years old, I got my passport, booked my ticket, got through customs, boarded the plane, and began my nineteen-hour journey to St. Petersburg, Russia. Landing there—the faces, the food, the culture, the language, the music, the rhythms of time, commuting—literally everything I knew was very different from what I had experienced before in my life, having been raised in a suburb of Atlanta, Georgia. During every exchange with others at the bus station, in a café, in the market, I found myself thinking, *Where I come from, we don't do it this way.* That's a bit of the experience that John has in mind here as he talks about this "kind of love."

John is getting at how alien, how foreign, how unique God's love is when compared to our limited, human, finite understandings of love! In his love, God not only covers our sin, but makes us part of his family! "God's love is foreign to humankind in that we cannot understand the magnitude of such love. It astonishes, amazes, and creates wonder within those who properly reflect upon it."[3] To be a child of God is not merely to be given a title; a child of God enjoys a living reality, a vibrant, authentic, passionate *relationship.*

### All God's Kids Call Him "Abba"

As a Christian, you've entered into a relationship with God that presses past knowing him as King, Creator, Judge, and Ruler over all things, and have come to know him in the most tender, dearest, most intimate and heart-moving way. You know him now as *Abba.* This little word only shows up three times in the New Testament, but don't let its brevity drive you to miss its immense importance.

As Jesus was praying in the garden of Gethsemane, sweating blood, knowing the brutal death that awaited him the following Friday morning, Mark writes, "Going a little farther, he fell on the ground and prayed that, if it were possible, the hour might pass from him. And he said, '*Abba*, Father, all things are possible for you. Remove this cup from me. Yet not what I will, but what you will'" (14:35–36). Paul uses the phrase two times. In Galatians 4:6 he writes, "Because you are his sons, God has sent the Spirit of his Son into our hearts, crying, '*Abba!* Father!'" And in Romans 8:15, he says, "You have received the Spirit of adoption as sons, by whom we cry, '*Abba!* Father!'"

Ronald Fung, research fellow of the Chinese University in Hong Kong, writes, "*Abba* is an Aramaic affectionate diminutive for 'father' used in the intimacy of the family circle."[4] Commenting on Galatians 4:6, Protestant reformer Martin Luther said, "Although I am oppressed with anguish and terror on every side, and seem to be forsaken and utterly cast away from Your presence, yet am I Your child, and You are my Father for Christ's sake; I am beloved because of the Beloved."[5] Luther understood that no matter what was going on in his life, one thing was certain—he was God's child.

The Christian God is three-in-one. Three distinct persons—Father, Son, and Holy Spirit—and yet One. This is known as the Trinity. Notice what Paul is saying in the Galatians reference; the Trinity is at work in this verse: God sent the Spirit of his Son into our hearts, crying, "*Abba!* Father!" Believer, prop up your feet in the hammock of the love of God for you. God does not disown his children, though his discipline can be quite painful at times. Because you are in Christ, you are just as safe, loved, and welcomed as Jesus is right now. Jesus has dealt with your sin at his cross, he has gifted to you his righteousness, and your identity is secure.

The craziest idea in the whole universe—that God cherishes you, sings over you, delights in you, and is wild over you being his child—is actually true! All the demons in hell, the liars in the streets, and even the deceptions of your own heart are no match for the landslide of the love of God that has broken loose for you. Nothing can quench the raging, blazing, longing heart of Almighty God! Your Abba will always be tender, truthful, and available to you.

## "In Christ" 240 Times!

As I stated earlier, you are not your status, your relationships, your income, or your job. You are not your current circumstances. You are not your failures, your successes, or your ambitions. You're not your GPA. You are not what your middle school coach or driver's ed teacher had to say about you. You are not what your critics say or what you think you are. You are who God says you are. But who does God say you are now that you're a Christian? More than that, did he say it clearly? The answer is a resounding *Yes!*

My fellow Christian, if God says one thing one time, it is important. If God repeats himself over and over again, then the issue must be of utmost importance; it isn't because God enjoys repeating himself or being redundant. It is because we desperately need to hear it. The short phrase *in Christ* describes what it means to be a Christian. In fact, this glorious phrase shows up 240 times in the New Testament! That's right. Over and over again, one of the ways the New Testament apostles discipled Christians was to remind them of their identity in Christ. According to the Bible, there are only two places a person can stand—either in Christ or outside of Christ. And you, as a Christian, are in Christ. You are loved, safe, and completely free. Yes, you are spotless, blameless, and at home in the family of God! This is the truest thing about you. You are one of God's beloved children.

### QUESTIONS TO CONSIDER

1. Why is it so important for Christians to truly understand that identity is received not achieved?

2. What does it mean to you to understand that you are a child of God?

3. How does it make you feel to know that God isn't your employer but is instead your Father?

# Quit Praying for God to Use You

*Real Relationship*

> We love those who know the worst of us and
> don't turn their faces away.
>
> —Walker Percy, *Love in the Ruins*

Steak filets and wine. Summer and swimming. Pollen and sneezing. Fire stations and Dalmatians. Kings and kingdoms. These all pair perfectly together for one reason or another. I want to talk about two major concepts presented in Scripture that will help make sense of the Christian faith—kingdom and covenant. I also want to bring in the practice of prayer as it relates to these two themes.

**Kingdom and Covenant**

The Bible uses all kinds of metaphors to describe our relationship with God and one another. You've probably heard of God referred to as "King" in a verse from the Bible, in a song, or in a prayer. You may have even heard that Jesus is the true "King of kings" (Revelation 19:16). Nowadays, in the West, we don't have kings and kingdoms, and that sometimes creates obstacles for us as we seek to understand the Bible. But don't worry! All is not lost! We just need to understand a few things. As a believer in Jesus, you must understand that coming into this kingdom is no small thing. The apostle Paul tells you, "You are not your own . . . you were bought with a price" (1 Corinthians 6:19–20).

Peter emphasizes just how high that price was to save your soul. He says,

> You were not bought with silver or gold money, which can spoil. You were bought with blood that is worth much. It is like the blood of a sheep that is perfect with nothing wrong in its body. You were bought with the blood of Christ.
>
> 1 Peter 1:18–19 WE

Because of what Jesus has done through his sacrificial death in your place for your sins (1 Corinthians 15:3), his resurrection from the dead (v. 4), and his faithfulness to send the Holy Spirit to indwell believers (Acts 2), you are now part of what the Bible calls the "kingdom of God"! Jesus himself speaks about the kingdom of God over *fifty* times in the Gospels.

### Road Sign: Heaven Ahead

What is this kingdom, exactly? Theologian Graeme Golds-worthy defines the kingdom of God as "God's people in God's place under God's rule."[1] God's people. God's place. God's rule. This speaks to our *relationship* with God. He is not only our Savior, he is also our Lord and our King. As Christians, we strive to live for the glory of our King in every area of life no matter what the culture says or how we are tempted. (More on this later.) The question beckons, "Is the kingdom *here and now* or is it somewhere far off in the future?" And the answer is *Yes.* One way theologians sometimes describe the kingdom of God is through using the acronym *ANY.* It stands for "Already, Not Yet."

The kingdom of God has broken into this world and is *already* here—God is reigning and ruling. *When* did the kingdom "break in"? Upon the resurrection and ascension of Jesus and his promise fulfilled in sending the Holy Spirit to indwell believers. As the children of God and citizens of this kingdom, we have a front-row seat as we witness just how great, how kind, how loving, how truthful, and powerful our God, our King, really is! We're getting real-life glimpses of what life will be like forever in heaven, our home.

Every minute of every day people are being healed, re-stored, loved, and welcomed into the family of God. As we read the Gospels, we encounter Jesus doing miracle after mir-acle—the blind are given their sight (John 9:1–12), the deaf are able to hear, the mute are able to speak (Mark 7:31–37), the sick are made well (Matthew 8:1–4), the hungry are fed

(John 6:1–15), the dead are raised to life (Mark 5:21–43), the lost are found, the spiritually dead are made alive (Luke 15:24)! It is helpful to remember that every time you see Jesus doing a miracle in the Bible it is like a sign on the Interstate saying, *This is what's coming!* For you and me, our next exit is heaven, our home—and at home, in our Father's house, all are made well, completely healed, totally loved, forever free to enjoy our heavenly Father! We will be part of a community completely void of racism, violence, negligence, and pain.

At the same time, it is also true that the kingdom is *not yet* here in its entirety. There are still so many that are broken and in need of God's saving and restoring. This is why the apostle John closes the Bible with the prayer "Come, Lord Jesus!" (Revelation 22:20). As a Christian, you are now a citizen of the household of God (Ephesians 2:19). You have been transferred out of the kingdom of darkness into the kingdom of his beloved Son (Colossians 1:13). And God, your King, did all of this through his power and his unending grace (Ephesians 2:8–10). This is how God has always done it—his people have always been brought into his family by his grace and through faith in him.

God spreads his kingdom much differently than the way other kings advance their reign. Earthly kings take more ground through power and force. God's kingdom moves forward every day, and yet it came at incredible cost to him through the death of Jesus. You and I are among those who were at one point his enemies, but are now his children (Romans 5:10), and nothing can or will ever change this reality. God considers you to be part of his covenant.

**Defining** *Covenant*

"What is a covenant?" you ask. Well, when we seek to define *covenant,* it can be a bit tricky. There is not really another word that gets at the heart of what is meant by covenant. *Covenant* is a special word, a sacred word, a holy word. For example, when two people get married, we don't say, "These two have entered into a legal contract." Rather, we say, "These two have made a covenant with each other." Covenantal language speaks of unbreakable, unending, unfading loving devotion and commitment.

God made many covenants with his people in the Bible. The covenants we see in the Old Testament are initiated by God and are made with people such as Noah, Abraham, Moses, and David. Rather than go into all the details of all the covenants, we will focus in on just one, the covenant with Abraham. You can read about Abraham's call and incredible story in the book of Genesis (particularly chapters 12–22). God appears to Abram (his birth name) in Genesis 12 and tells him to leave his family, his country, his predictable life and *go.* Abram doesn't know exactly where he is to go, and God says, "I will show you" (Genesis 12:1). So Abram took his wife Sarai and his nephew Lot, and went. God promised to give Abram a son, and told him that eventually all the peoples of the world would be blessed through him, and that his descendants would outnumber the stars in the sky. When Abram wonders how he will know all of this will come to pass, God answers by making a covenant with him.

How this comes about sounds strange to you and me. In the West, we sign contracts with ink. In the Ancient Near

East, blood was involved. God told Abram to gather a heifer, a goat, a ram, a turtledove, and a young pigeon, slaughter them, and cut them in half. In that culture, in a typical covenant ceremony, the animals would be cut in half and the two parties would pass through the middle of the pieces. The passing through would signify a statement to each party to the effect that "If I don't honor my word, my commitment, my covenant with you, may my body end up like these animals."

Wouldn't you agree that blood speaks louder than ink? However, that evening something completely unexpected happened. A smoking firepot and flaming torch passed between the pieces. It was the Lord God himself who passed through. What did that say to Abram? God was saying, "I will be faithful to you no matter the cost." This is grace.

## Covenant vs. Contract

A covenant isn't just different from a contract; it is the *opposite* of a contract. Contractual relationships say, "I'm committed to the following items and no more." More than that, a contract communicates that "if you fail to live up to any of these expectations, the contract is terminated and penalties will be enforced." But God didn't draft a contract with Abram or with you. God entered a covenant, saying, "I'm committed to your good no matter how many times you fail, how many times you break my heart. I will lovingly abide with you through unmet expectations. I will bleed for this." And he did. That's God's heart toward his children. The cross of Jesus communicates that not only is God disinterested in a contract, the very idea of a works-based relationship repulses him. He is totally committed in *covenantal* love. Contracts are easy. Covenants are more involved. Contracts make sense to the average person. Covenants aren't always understood, especially by unbelievers. Contracts don't involve your soul. Covenants do. God has made a covenant with his children.

As I have said before, you are not God's employee. You are not God's hired hand. God is not a CEO who never makes his way down the assembly line to get to know the people who were hired to work day after day. The banner that flies over your life is love. You are God's child. You are God's chosen. You are God's elect son or daughter. Believe this: All the water in all the oceans could never extinguish the fire of God's love for you.

If you don't understand your true identity as being deeply loved by God and secure in his covenant, you'll be bound for an unbelievably long road called "your Christian faith." Perhaps a brief illustration will help. I've worked all kinds of jobs, from manual labor, to retail, to serving tables in restaurants. At one point during my seminary days, I worked two jobs and sometimes three in order to pay for my classes. For my third job, I was a day-laborer. I'd appear at a gas station early in the morning, hang out with a huge number of other men, and wait for some guy to show up in a big truck, look over the crowd, and pick up a couple of us to do landscaping or some other kind of manual labor. I knew if I was chosen I'd make at least $100 for my day's work. I'd hop in the truck with a stranger and go to a work site. He'd tell me what to do, and then at the end of the workday, he'd take me back to the gas station and drop me off, never to talk to me again. Some Christians think God is like that. He simply picks you up to go to work with no intention of developing a relationship with you. But that's not even close to the heart of God!

God has called us to intimacy with himself as a loving Father to his child. God has called you into a relationship with him that is initiated by unconditional love and filled with grace and truth. So don't sell yourself short and merely stand by the fire of God's love. Step into it, take the step of faith toward vulnerability with the One who created you, loved you, and moved heaven and earth to be with you. Let his love define your relationship, and you'll burn, you'll glow, you'll be the light of the world that Jesus said you were meant to be.

## God Is Far More Relational Than Utilitarian

I quite literally grew up in the church, and for that I am eternally grateful! The name of Jesus and the word *gospel* are as familiar to me as *Mom* and *Dad*. By now, I must have seen more than a thousand people baptized and heard countless sermons. Mission work, Christian literature, and being involved in the church have always been a part of my life, and I wouldn't change any of it. When I was younger, I heard evangelists who came to our church and talked about the drugs they did and the poor decisions they made before meeting Jesus. I thought, *I'll never have a testimony as cool as that. Drugs. Jail time. Rock bottom. Stealing cars. All I am is an average kid growing up in the suburbs who goes to church every week.* Nowadays, I pray for my kids to have a "boring" testimony. I'd love for my kids to be able to say, "Yeah, we grew up going to church. Daddy was a pastor. I met Jesus at a young age and always walked with him." I'll take that testimony for my children any day. My assumption is that you would too.

I deeply love the church. I have given my life to the planting of churches and raising up leaders within those churches. I simply cannot imagine my life without the local church and the invaluable role it has played. Though churches can be messy, it is clear to me that God has not given up on the church, but rather loves and inhabits it. The church is what Jesus gave his life for, and therefore, the church is what I am giving my life to loving, building, and serving.

I became a Christian at the age of fifteen, and knew I was called into vocational ministry within ninety days. One prayer that I picked up from leaders and mentors around me and started praying for myself was this: *God, please use me in this world for your glory and our joy.* It sounds right, and even biblical. We have commands like "Whatever you do, do all to the glory of God" (1 Corinthians 10:31). And Paul told the Ephesians, "We are God's work of art, created in Christ Jesus for the good works which God has already designated to make up our way of life" (2:10 NJB). I wanted to live for God's glory and go about doing the good works that I had been created to do.

I still feel this way, but have had to go through some changes in my motivation. To be quite honest, I didn't pray that prayer from a heart that was content with God. I prayed that prayer because I wanted to perform for God, others, and myself. I wanted God to give me a platform, put me in front of people who would laud me with praises and admire my piety. True story. (I'm sure those who know me are grinning.) I equated godliness with getting attention. I thought Christlikeness was found on a stage. I thought being Spirit-filled would make me bold in preaching and in conversation. Little did I know that sometimes the boldest thing I could do was to listen.

I still have all of my old journals. They're embarrassing to read, partly because of my age and general immaturity at the time. But more than that, my gross pietism, legalism, and desperate need to be liked and noticed by successful religious people is actually nauseating to me now. When I wrote the words, I thought they were filled with wisdom and profound insights. Turns out, I may be the greatest navel-gazer in the history of the world. Every couple of years, I pull the journals down to read in order to see if I've grown much, if any, in my walk with God. The one phrase that is on every page is *Use me*. To me, that is really sad. Here's why: I've come to believe that God is far more *relational* than utilitarian. God did not save me so that he could merely use me. He saved me by his grace and for his glory. He saved me for a relationship with him.

Some of us learn things the hard way. For over a decade, I thought that if I turned up the disciplines of working hard, praying consistently, and memorizing pounds of Scripture that somehow I would turn God's head, get his attention, impress him, and even cause him to love me. Then I realized that it is his kindness that leads to repentance (Romans 2:4) and that I'm not a summation of my good days or bad days but I am "in Christ." Letting God love me as I am without masks, costumes, or religious disguises has changed me in more ways than I ever imagined. In fact, the things I used to call "disciplines" are becoming more natural rhythms (even habits!) because my identity has been fundamentally altered by encountering God on his terms, not mine.

The obvious rebuttal would be "Oh! But you were 'created in Christ Jesus for good works'!" (Ephesians 2:10). And I could not love that verse more! However, chronology counts, and chapter 1 of Ephesians comes before chapter 2. My huge error has been to study, ponder, and dissect chapter 1 and want to *apply* chapter 2. But I need to apply chapter 1 first. In Ephesians 1, Paul says, "In love he predestined us for adoption as sons" (v. 4–5). That changes everything! That verse causes Christians to debate, argue, and divide over predestination, the will of God, and the free will of man. But rather than argue, I encourage you to focus on the "in love" portion of the verses. God loves you. He wanted you as one of his children.

My wife, Jana, and I did not choose to have children in order to "use them." We did not have them so that we could accomplish our purpose in the world through them. In other words, we did not have children as a means to an end. We had children in order to love them, teach them, and bless them. We wanted them. The older I get, the more I become convinced that the love motive is nearer to the heart of God.

My confession is simple: Deep down, for the majority of my Christian life, I have lived, prayed, and served because I related to God as my employer, not my "*Abba,* Father" (Galatians 4:6; Romans 8:15). With God as my divine employer, I could count and quantify my work for him and be the judge of whether or not I was useful to him. How many doors did I knock on? How many people made decisions for Christ after my sermon? How many people attended my church? How much money was raised? And on and on this accounting went.

Relating to God as my employer or my "boss," as I recently heard an evangelist describe him, had a catastrophic impact on how I understood myself and others in the world. When it came to love, intimacy, acceptance, and belonging in the family of God, I only felt like those experiences were appropriate if I was performing well enough. Diligent Bible study, punctual giving on the first and fifteenth of the month, incessant prayer, yearly foreign mission trips, and being at church every time the doors were open was the name of the game. Without being able to quantify my hours, events, and dollars, how in the world would I know where I stood with God?

Somehow, the cross of Jesus faded into the background. Somewhere along the way, Jesus' statement "It is finished" was turned into a memorial instead of a living reality. The gospel says, "It is finished." But what I really heard was "You must finish it." I knew in theory that I was saved by grace, but I thought it was my responsibility to keep my seat at the table. Productivity and getting things done were most important. Meditation, confession, and repentance were replaced with planning, strategizing, and mission. Furthermore, with a divine employer, it was easy to compare and compete with other Christians, whom I saw as fellow employees jockeying for a better position. As I measured myself against other Christians or students in Bible college and seminary, a secret pride in my heart robbed me of authentic friendships that include transparency and gut-wrenching vulnerability. When

I was broken, at my lowest, I found out just how consumer-based my relationships were. I needed family, not co-workers, to comfort me, and I had none.

I've wondered why I tried to create a wobbly platform or climb the rickety ladder in evangelical circles so many days of my Christian faith. I've come to conclude and repent of the fact that I'd rather study the love of God than be consumed by it, thinking about the love of God rather than actually *feeling* loved by God felt safe. Like so many Christians I know, I would rather forego my daddy issues and sweep my own brokenness under the rug. I'd rather look like I have it all together and get on to the "good works prepared for me." My struggle is not with being productive in the work of the church. Rather, my struggle has been to actually see myself as one of God's children based solely on the work of his Son, the Lord Jesus. To believe that God wants me, loves me, and totally accepts me apart from my performance is where it all gets real. Distinguishing myself from my wins and losses and getting my identity from Jesus alone is where Christianity starts to feel real.

In the most powerful anthropomorphic language in the Bible, God confirms that he is far more relational than utilitarian. In Isaiah 49:15–16, God compares himself to a nursing mother with her child. In Hosea 11:1–4, 8, he is a daddy teaching his toddler to walk by taking him up by his little arms. In Jeremiah 31:20, the Father says, "Is not Israel still my son, my darling child?"

Do I want to be used by God in this world? I think that's the wrong question. Will I have the nerve to go beyond studying the love of God and allow God to love me in such a way that I feel his love in this world? If so, I'm certain that walking in the good works prepared for me won't feel so much like work, but in and of itself will feel much more like the reward, because I'm going to work with my Abba Father. Bottom line—God has children, not employees. God gives us a covenant, not a contract. God pours out love, not busywork. I confess all of this here so that you won't go down the long, unnecessary road of relating to God as an employee, and so that you'll enjoy what it is to be one of his children.

### QUESTIONS TO CONSIDER

1. What does it mean to be part of the kingdom of God?
2. In your own words, define the word *covenant*.
3. What is the benefit of knowing that you are one of God's children instead of an employee? Why is it so important to understand this?

# Don't Fake It With God

*Real Prayer*

> To pray is to listen to the One who calls you
> "my beloved daughter," "my beloved son," "my
> beloved child."
>
> —Henri Nouwen

"Fake it till you make it" is a common cliché. The silly expression encourages us to put up a front, to act like we know what we're doing, or that we're enjoying ourselves in whatever circumstance we find ourselves until things eventually go our way. We've all faked it at some point in our lives so as not to stand out, rock the boat, or run the risk of total embarrassment.

Why do we do things like this? Is it because we can't stand the awkward squirming that accompanies truth, honesty, and vulnerability? If we don't fake it, we run the risk of rejection.

Thus we pretend to enjoy ourselves. And this is not only something we do in relation to family, friends, and strangers; we're tempted to do the same with God, who knows all and sees all things (Hebrews 4:13).

But God is not dull, plastic, or hollow. He knows every detail about you and me (Psalm 139). God does not create the inauthentic. He has no interest in your faking your way through this thing called Christianity. Your relationship with God, though free to you, came at incalculable expense to him. The sinless life, brutal death, and triumphant resurrection of Jesus Christ are the gifts that grant us access to God. When tempted to doubt whether God understands what we're going through, or when we think we may have gone too far for him to be willing to hear our prayers, we must remind ourselves what the author of Hebrews says:

> We do not have a high priest who is unable to empathize with our weaknesses, but we have one who has been tempted in every way, just as we are—yet he did not sin. Let us then approach God's throne of grace with confidence, so that we may receive mercy and find grace to help us in our time of need.
>
> 4:15–16 NIV

You have a perfect Savior who understands every aspect of your life. Notice his position. When it comes to his children, he is not dressed for battle, set to attack. Rather, he is seated on a throne of pure, inexhaustible grace. God wants the real you and nothing less than you, pouring out your heart before him regardless of what state or condition it may be in. In fact, this is where we see theology born and take shape.

Henri Nouwen writes,

> The original meaning of the word *theology* was 'union with
> God in prayer.' Today theology has become one academic
> discipline alongside many others, and often theologians
> are finding it hard to pray.[1]

He wants *all* of you and nothing less. This includes the really
*passionate* parts of you, the *vulnerable* parts, the *emotional* parts,
the *truest* parts of you—the *real* you. To put it bluntly, Jesus did
not go through the horrors of Calvary, burst out of the grave
on Easter morning, and send the Holy Spirit to indwell you
all so that you could *fake it* in your relating to God.

So before we take one more step into this chapter about
prayer, may I suggest that you take a moment and pray something along these lines:

> *God, I'm here with you, and this book talking to me about*
> *talking to you. I am joining the disciples, who asked Jesus*
> *how to pray. Teach me to wait, to listen, to talk, request,*
> *and even call out desperately from time to time. Guide me,*
> *convict me, encourage me, and dwell with me. Teach me to*
> *pray. Thank you, Jesus, for making this moment possible.*
> *Father, I am yours, come what may. Amen.*

As a professing Christian, you've already made some pretty
enormous steps of faith. You believe that God exists. You
believe that Jesus has the power to conquer your greatest
fears, take away all of your guilt and shame, and has given to
you his righteousness free of charge! You believe that God

the Holy Spirit indwells you, leads you, guides you, convicts you, and comforts you. You believe that the Bible is the Word of God. You believe that you have eternal life given to you now and that your place in heaven is not wishful thinking. It is the surest reality! Additionally, you believe that God is *relational*—that you can relate to him and that he relates to *you, personally.* With all of these beliefs in place, why settle, as so many do, for a mediocre relationship with God Almighty? *This chapter is all about exploring an authentic relationship with God through prayer.* Be encouraged as you continue on your journey with Jesus.

### "Teach Us to Pray"

Though an oftentimes difficult group of men, the disciples managed on more than one occasion to ask questions and make requests of Jesus that you and I are still benefiting from to this very hour. Just think, where would we be without the disciples asking Jesus, "Lord, teach us to pray" (Luke 11:1)? What a *brilliant* request of the disciples that they be instructed in the art, the craft, the discipline, and *relational* gold mine known as *prayer*! Apparently, they needed to be taught how to pray (as do we). It was quite appropriate for the disciples to approach their rabbi and seek instruction. Not only did they know Jesus as "Rabbi" (or "Teacher") in title, they observed Jesus living out his theology of prayer regularly. The Gospels show us that Jesus prayed repeatedly in any and every situation. Have you ever wondered what it's actually supposed to look like to have a *real* relationship with God? What images come to mind? A monk in a monastery? A priest in a confessional? An elderly woman in a church pew? A fiery preacher leading an altar call? Maybe pure boredom comes to mind.

As the Son of God, Jesus was equal with God (John 5:18) and perfectly demonstrated in real space and time what an authentic, unbroken relationship with God the Father actually looks like. Paul tells us that we are to "pray without ceasing" (1 Thessalonians 5:17). But what is prayer, exactly? What is the point of praying? What does it accomplish? Of course, one short chapter in a small book cannot possibly exhaust all there is to say about prayer. So this chapter is going to focus on the relationship we have with God more than anything else.

**Prayer Is Relational**

Preacher and writer A.W. Tozer wrote, "What comes into our minds when we think about God is the most important thing about us."[2] In the gospel, we learn that we need not be unnecessarily afraid of God or avoid him, but should approach him regularly in prayer (Matthew 6:9–13). God is holy, but we need not run from him! All of our sins are separated from us, and we are seen as Christ is—blameless, holy, and loved. We have a Father who protects us, not a bully who taunts us. We have a King who leads us, not a boss who badgers us. We have a Savior who keeps us, not a friend who abandons us. God cherishes his children. How you think about God will determine the quality and frequency of your prayers to him.

Prayer is something that is practiced in virtually every religion in some form or another. As relational beings, humans long to feel and be connected to themselves, others, and ultimately, their god. And yet, unlike other religions, the Christian faith erupts on the scene with something that isn't found anywhere else. As the children of God, we experience something of unparalleled significance—knowing God closely. There is real intimacy, a warmness between children crying out, "Abba! Father!" (Galatians 4:6), and his responding in love.

And yet, while we enjoy this free access to our heavenly Father, if there is one thing that is consistent across the board with Christians, it is that we *all* struggle at various times and ways with our prayer life (pastors, theologians, and the giants of church history included!). You see, prayer is neither easy nor difficult all the time. At its core, prayer is relational, which means that it must be looked after, tended to, and cared for, much like a garden.

### The Lord's Prayer

Probably the most famous prayer in the Christian faith is known as the Lord's Prayer. It is recorded in two of the four gospels (Matthew and Luke), and they differ slightly. Below we will look at what Matthew has for us, being that his is the more popular version. This prayer has served to guide, instruct, and challenge Christians all over the globe for more than two thousand years. The words contained here are real, authentic, sobering, and full of grace and truth. The content of the prayer is as theologically rich as anything else in the Bible, and yet, it is a prayer that is understood and offered in complete simplicity. Jesus, in this prayer, is giving us a glimpse into how to think about and commune with God. Prayer is a two-way street. We speak to God, and God speaks to us. In this prayer, God is worshiped, sins are confessed, requests for provisions are made, as the child of God engages the heart of God.

For all the well-meaning how-to books on prayer, I, along with many others, have experienced frustration, because trying to apply someone else's rigid routine feels awkward or inauthentic. John Chapman encourages people to "Pray as you can and do not try to pray as you can't."[3] He's getting at this idea of an authentic relationship with God. Jesus instructs us:

> Pray then like this: "Our Father in heaven, hallowed be your name. Your kingdom come, your will be done, on earth as it is in heaven. Give us this day our daily bread, and forgive us our debts, as we also have forgiven our debtors. And lead us not into temptation, but deliver us from evil."
>
> —Matthew 6:9–13

Here are just a few things to note as you journey through this prayer.

### Our Father in heaven, hallowed be your name

To begin with, Jesus uses the pronoun *our* instead of *my*. This points to the fact that our faith is a family faith, something that is shared with many others. You have been welcomed into the family of God. Just as there is no such thing as a single individual who comprises a family, so it is in the church.

Next, Jesus tells us to go before God, calling him *Father*. This isn't to downplay God as Creator, King, Lord, Judge, and

Master, but rather it establishes the tender relationship that is shared between God and his people. To go before God as your heavenly Father in prayer is to approach the One who holds all things together, is perfect in wisdom, unrivaled in strength, and full of incomprehensible love. He will always welcome you kindly. A good father does what is right and good for the child even when the child doesn't think it so. We must remember that God is not a cosmic Santa Claus, but is our heavenly Father. As we approach our Father in heaven and pray, it is important to know that "God will either give us what we ask or give us what we would have asked if we knew everything he knew."[4]

Jesus also locates the Father in heaven: high, exalted, lifted up, reigning and ruling. God the Father is close, immanent, and intimate with his children. And yet, he is in heaven, which communicates that he is also holy, transcendent, and the sovereign king of all creation.

The word *hallow* is an old word that really isn't used anymore, and yet it still lingers on in many modern translations of the Bible. To hallow something means to make it of first importance, one's highest priority. Jesus teaches us to pray that God's name, his character, his will, his fame, would take preeminence before everything else in our lives.

### Your kingdom come, your will be done, on earth as it is in heaven

This means that we long to see God bring what happens in his "living room" in heaven to our living rooms, our streets, our cities, and this whole world. This is a prayer asking God to do things his way in this world. Essentially, we are asking

God to extend his rule over every aspect of creation. And because *we* are praying this, we are seeking to align ourselves with and participate in this reality.

### Give us this day our daily bread

This is a prayer for God's constant provision for our everyday needs. As Christians, we believe that we are not the ones who provide for ourselves. Rather, we continue to go before God, who cares deeply for us, seeking his good provisions.

### And forgive us our debts, as we also have forgiven our debtors

Christians are not sinless; Jesus is. Sin, at its core, breaks relationships. And Jesus teaches us that we are to bring our sins before God and ask his forgiveness. We do this in order to remain in an ongoing state of abiding with God (John 15:2) and being reconciled with him (2 Corinthians 5:18). God is compassionate and merciful and thus by his very nature he "bears with and forgives people's twisting his words and will. [He] endures breaches of trust by persons with whom he has a relationship and suffers the missing of the goals he sets for his people."[5] John reminds us, "If we confess our sins, he is faithful and just to forgive us our sins and cleanse us from all unrighteousness" (1 John 1:9).

### And lead us not into temptation, but deliver us from evil

Thousands of pages have been labored over for the last two thousand years examining just what is going on in this request. Could God possibly lead us into sinning? Or is the word *temptation* to be understood in light of *testing* us? The summary I've come across that best helps me understand what is going on here comes from theologian Don Carson. He thinks that it is what is referred to as a *litotes*, which is a way of affirming something while stating its opposite. For example, "You won't regret going to eat at Fogo De Chao" is the same as saying, "You're really going to enjoy eating at Fogo De Chao." Carson says:

> "Into temptation" is negated: Lead us, *not* into temptation, but away from it, into righteousness, into situations where far from being tempted, we will be protected and therefore kept righteous. As the second clause of this petition expresses it, we will then be delivered from the evil one.[6]

A growing Christian is a repenting Christian. Repentance involves more than changing your mind about something you've done or feeling remorse over sin. Repentance means to agree with God about sin, grieve over committing sin, and then walk in the opposite direction of sin. Praying to be continually delivered from temptation is absolutely imperative for the growing believer. Commenting on this section of Scripture, New Testament historian N. T. Wright says,

> Jesus' resurrection is the beginning of God's new project not to snatch people away from earth to heaven but to colonize earth with the life of heaven. That, after all, is what the Lord's Prayer is about.[7]

## Bored in Prayer

Depending on just how new you are to the Christian faith, you may or may not have been told that sometimes when we go to pray we can find ourselves in a place of distraction or even plain boredom. There will be times that feel as though your relationship with God is going nowhere or, at best, progressing at a snail's pace. Christians sometimes go through long seasons in which things are dry, God seems distant, and talking to the wall will appear more productive than praying. This happens from time to time to everyone. It is normal. But *when* that day comes, remind yourself that the problem is most certainly not with God. God is not boring. The problem is that we lack wonder. And here's what's great: God's faithfulness to us is not contingent on whether or not we are bored or blown away with God.

Do you ever fall asleep praying? How bad do you feel when that happens? In college, I was telling my roommate that I felt so guilty for falling asleep praying at night. I was up at four a.m., trying my hardest to get in a few hours of prayer and Bible study before the school day began, so by the time I was saying my bedtime prayers, I was exhausted. True story.

"I wouldn't fall asleep talking to the president. How in the world can I fall asleep talking to God?" I said to my roommate.

He asked, "Isn't God your Father?"

"Yes," I replied.

"Do you want to have children someday?"

"Yeah, I do. Why?"

He said, "Well, can you imagine what it will be like to have your little boy come in from preschool, tell you all about his day, thank you for playing with him, and for his toys, ask for you to help him with something tomorrow, say that he loves you, and fall asleep on your chest while he's talking? How would you feel about your son?"

I finally got it! That day everything began to change about my prayer life. And that's not sloppy sentimentalism. That's gospel. You see, while God is the Judge of the universe, his children know that his throne is, above all, a throne of grace, and they have received a warm invitation to come and be with him.

And while God is our tender Father, we need not mistake his kindness for naïveté. The lamb is also the lion, and it is so important that we remember just how great, strong, and limitless our Father really is, for it changes how we relate to him and what we communicate to him. The God you now know and worship through Jesus isn't common, trite, or boring. He is not hurting for power, knowledge, wealth, or fame. He is still the unrivaled, unmatched, undefeated King of kings and Lord of lords (1 Timothy 6:15; Revelation 19:6). He has no beginning and no end (Psalm 90:2). He has no birthday or expiration date. God is as secure as he's ever been (50:12). No one goes before him, and there is no suitable follow-up to his reign. God is his own origin, his own footnote, his own self-worth.

The earth is his footstool (Isaiah 66:1). Innumerable angels are his servants (Hebrews 12:22). Everything created exists for his glory (Romans 11:36)! The farthest star in the most distant galaxy burns for him this very second. The speed of the cheetah; the textures in an elephant's tusk; the burning purple, red, and gold colors of the Gold Coast in Australia; the scales on the back of a copperhead; the kaleidoscopic shapes in the spider web on the back porch, filled with hundreds of water beads after a drizzly day in Seattle; the eerily gorgeous sci-fi greens and blues and yellows of the northern lights put on display around the Arctic Circle; the wind in a pine tree; the ever so complex endoplasmic reticulum of a cell; and the late-night coo of a newborn baby are all telling of his creative majesty! His sidewalks are paved in gold (Revelation. 21:21). His voice shakes the heavens and the earth (Hebrews 12:26).

Christian, consider that our God has never known a moment of need, anxiety, or fear. Time itself is outside of and subject to him. The mightiest kingdom is but a grain of sand in his palm. The finest musicians the world has ever produced have yet to compose something fit for *this* King (Psalm 8). Of all the artwork created across the globe—beginning with the Neanderthal's etchings on a cave wall to the works of Michelangelo, Monet, Dali, and beyond—all of the colors, shapes, textures, and tones are but whispers of this King of Glory. Sculptors cannot mold him. Architects cannot build a tower up to him (Genesis 11). Engineers cannot design anything like him (Exodus 20). The most cathartic of poets cannot stir the emotions high enough, deep enough, or wide enough for our God. Theologians study, stutter, stammer, and fall all over themselves like toddlers when seeking to speak of him.

The Bible teaches us that out of sheer grace, God wants a real relationship with you, and one of the primary ways in which this relationship is built will be over a lifetime of prayer. Sometimes these prayers will go on for hours. Other times, there will only be a sentence muttered, and sometimes even less, just a single word like *"Help!"* In fact, "Perhaps the shortest and most powerful prayer in the human language is *help*."[8]

We need to be assured that God hears our prayers (Psalm 6:9), is lacking nothing (50:8), and is most certainly gentle with his children; after all, the Holy Spirit is known as our Helper (John 16:7) or Comforter, in other Bible translations. What comes to your mind when you think of God really matters. But what if boredom isn't the issue? What happens when we're angry with God?

## Yelling at God/Pouring Out Complaint

The Bible gives us many examples of God's people laying it all out on the table. The best place to go in Scripture to see examples of this is the Psalms. Look at these verses:

> With my voice I cry out to the Lord; with my voice I plea for mercy to the Lord. I pour out my complaint before him; I declare my trouble before him.

> Psalm 142:1–2

Or consider that we are to:

> Trust in him at all times, O people; pour out your heart before him; God is a refuge for us. *Selah.*

> Psalm 62:8

Or consider these nine verses and see the absolute gut-wrenching vulnerability of the psalmist here:

> I cry out to God; yes, I shout.
>     Oh, that God would listen to me!

When I was in deep trouble,
　　I searched for the Lord.
All night long I prayed, with hands lifted toward heaven,
　　but my soul was not comforted.
I think of God, and I moan,
　　overwhelmed with longing for his help. *Interlude*

You don't let me sleep.
　　I am too distressed even to pray!
I think of the good old days,
　　long since ended,
when my nights were filled with joyful songs.
　　I search my soul and ponder the difference now.
Has the Lord rejected me forever?
　　Will he never again be kind to me?
Is his unfailing love gone forever?
　　Have his promises permanently failed?
Has God forgotten to be gracious?
　　Has he slammed the door on his compassion?

Psalm 77:1–9 NLT

Christians are to turn first and most often to God to declare, complain, and pour out our troubles. This doesn't negate the necessity of pastors and counselors and community. However, even the best of people are still just people. God alone is our salvation, and it is ultimately Jesus who lifts our burdens. It is to him that we are to bring our anxieties, rolling them onto his shoulders (1 Peter 5:7). After all, "A child cannot do a bad coloring; nor can a child of God do bad prayer."[9]

In the movie *The Apostle*, Robert Duvall portrays Sonny, a southern pastor as raw as they come in his relationship with

God. The story goes that Sonny has a successful ministry, but then the most unexpected turn of his life happens: his wife cheats on him with another man. Sonny, filled with rage, loses his mind, hunts the man down at a children's baseball game, and strikes the man with a baseball bat, killing him. Sonny then flees town and goes to live in a rural place with his mother. Late one night, Sonny goes up into the attic of his mother's house and shouts in uncensored honesty. This is most definitely not a prayer that you'd find in any church service. In all of his pain, his confusion, his total anger with the shape of his life, his broken dreams, and cluttered head, Sonny's passion-filled and completely disoriented heart comes up through his mouth and belts at the top of his lungs:

> Somebody, I say, somebody has taken my wife; they've stolen my church! That's the temple I built for you! I'm gonna yell at you 'cause I'm mad at you! I can't take it!
>
> Give me a sign or somethin'. Blow this pain out of me. Give it to me tonight, Lord God Jehovah. If you won't give me back my wife, give me peace. Give it to me, give it to me, give it to me, give it to me. Give me peace. Give me peace.
>
> I don't know who's been foolin' with me—you or the Devil. I don't know. And I won't even bring the human into this—he's just a mutt—so I'm not even gonna bring him into it. But I'm confused. I'm mad. I love you, Lord, I love you, but I'm mad at you. I am mad at you!
>
> So deliver me tonight, Lord. What should I do? Now tell me. Should I lay hands on myself? What should I do? I know I'm a sinner and once in a while a womanizer, but I'm your servant! Ever since I was a little boy and you brought me back from the dead, I'm your servant! What should I

do? Tell me. I've always called you Jesus; you've always called me Sonny. What should I do, Jesus? This is Sonny talkin' now.

Just then the phone rings; a neighbor calls complaining to Sonny's mother about the noise. His mother replies, "Sometimes Sonny talks to the Lord and sometimes he yells at the Lord. Tonight he happens to be yelling at him."[10]

The reality is that God is not afraid of you, your fears, your frustrations, or your anger. That's right. God can put up with all of your anger at him and still keep that same look of loving, longing compassion for you. He knows you. So feel free as you bow your knees, to let your hair down, too, and join Sonny in a dose of authenticity.

### QUESTIONS TO CONSIDER

1. What have you learned so far about prayer?
2. Do you ever get bored in prayer? If so, what do you do?
3. How often do you pray?
4. Have you ever been so mad at God that you let him have it like Sonny?

# REAL OBEDIENCE

When Christ calls a man, he bids him come
and die. It may be a death like that of the first
disciples who had to leave home and work to
follow him, or it may be a death like Luther's,
who had to leave the monastery and go out
into the world. But it is the same death every
time—death in Jesus Christ, the death of the
old man at his call.

—Dietrich Bonhoeffer, *The Cost of Discipleship*

For all that has changed as a result of becoming a Christian,
the temptation to sin doesn't just vanish, as you've probably
noticed. Countless things will change because you've met
Jesus. But the temptation to fulfill your own vision for your
life and the pure ignorance that indwells all of us, believing
that God is somehow still holding out on us, doesn't change.
This doesn't mean that you haven't grown and won't continue

to grow. You have and you will. Yet sin is deceptive (Hebrews 3:13) and comes in many forms throughout our lives. What you're struggling with today may not be what you'll be facing a year, two years, or fifty years from now. I don't say that to discourage you. I say that to help you have a clear, sober assessment of what it looks like to know and walk with Jesus in this world.

So yes, you're a new creation (2 Corinthians 5:17). Yes, you have the Holy Spirit indwelling you (John 15). No, you are no longer "enslaved to sin" (Romans 6:6) and now "have become [a slave] of righteousness" (6:18). But the desires of the flesh, the lust of the eyes, and the pride of life (1 John 2:16) are still very real things, and as followers of Jesus, we must battle against these at all costs! The lust, the greed, the pride, the constant posturing and positioning to make ourselves look better than we are is the stuff in us that we have to die to *daily*. Brennan Manning said it this way: "The temptation to look good without being good is the temptation of the age."[1] Believe me. He's right.

You may be wondering, *Does the temptation ever go away?* The answer is no. Not yet, anyway. That day is still to come. Right now, we fight the good fight. This chapter is about going to war against sin and pursuing obedience to God. In theological terms, the process of becoming more like Jesus is known as *sanctification*. This is where Christians lose popularity points, big time, with those who don't follow Jesus— because while Jesus certainly loves the people of the world, he does not love every idea, practice, habit, and action *in* the world. And we are called to walk after him every step of the way, knowing that we will be hated for it. And yet, we joy-fully proceed in light of the fact that the King of the universe is our Father and he's given us a family called "the church." This family understands the journey we're on, the fight we're in, the life we're living, because they, like us, are in it, too.

With that said, let's start with the hard stuff—the heart. The reason, the motivation, the drive behind *why* we seek to put our sin to death is not to impress a religious crowd or earn the love of God. We pursue God's will because the love and glory of God has captivated us, and it simply looks better, tastes better, and is more satisfying than anything this world has to offer. At the end of the day, the world is hand-ing out fake pearls, knock-off sunglasses, and cheap sex. In contrast, the God of the universe extends to us abundant and eternal life. Not only that, he's a happy God. And he offers his love, not generic sentimentalism and cheap Valentine's Day chocolate, but covenantal love, signed in his own blood. That, my brothers and sisters, is *why* we take up our cross and follow Jesus wherever he leads. Let's dive in.

## Good Guys and Bad Guys

Many Christians live their entire lives under the impression that the Bible has two teams: winners and losers, good guys and bad guys, saints and sinners. The good guys naturally obey God, always do the right thing, never get out of line, hold doors for women, and tip waitresses well. They're the great examples for us to follow. They're courteous in traffic, nice to children, keep a close eye on their waistline, and root for the home team. They're quick to say "Excuse me," arrive early, and smile wide at strangers.

The bad guys are those who sin a lot, screw up everything, have bad attitudes, terrible breath, and repeatedly make a mess out of whatever situation they find themselves in because they're *bad*. Therefore, the big idea is to try to be a good guy with good morals, not a bad guy with bad morals. We could call this a "moralistic" reading of the Bible, as the aim of Bible study is to look for the moral of the story and try your best to abide by it. However, that is an over-simplified and completely incorrect view of both the message and the characters in the Bible. Don't believe me? Here are some examples of how popular moralistic readings of the Bible fall apart:

*Moralism says:* "Be patient like Sarah, who waited so long for Isaac to be born." But the Bible also says that she was faithless and even laughed at God's audacious promise to give an old woman a baby.

*Moralism says:* "Be like Noah, who had great faith to build the ark." But the Bible says that after getting off the boat, he got drunk and passed out naked in front of his family.

*Moralism says:* "Be like Moses: a bold, faithful, and brave leader." But the Bible says that Moses murdered a man, looked for excuses not to obey God, and lost his temper with God and people on more than one occasion.

*Moralism says:* "Be like David, who loved God very much, killed Goliath, and led the nation." But the Bible says that

David committed adultery and had Bathsheba's husband, Uriah, murdered.

*Moralism says:* "Be like Peter, who preached boldly at Pentecost." But we forget that Peter denied Jesus three times and even later on as a pastor struggled with being a people pleaser and had to be corrected by Paul.

Speaking of Paul, *moralism says:* "Be like the brave, faithful, and courageous missionary, Paul." But remember, before Paul met Jesus, he too consented to and oversaw the execution of Christians, confessed that he struggled daily with sin, and even understood himself to be the "chief of sinners."

And on and on it goes. A moralistic reading of the Bible is not simply one small error when it comes to reading our Bible—it misses the entire point of the Bible! What are we supposed to do when we discover that the good guys are actually the bad guys, too? Despair? No! We're left with the question: "Has anyone lived a good, perfect, blameless, and righteous life before God?" The Bible comes back with the loud answer: "Yes! There is one!" His name is Jesus. And as Christians, we are to follow him as our Savior and Lord.

## Jesus Is Better Than Superman

In the Old Testament, God liberated his people and gave them specific commands to abide by. This foreshadowed what was to come in Christ. In the Old Testament, God's people understood him to be their Savior and Lord. The same is true in the New Testament. Jesus' dominion expands far beyond the borders of Israel, as he is declared to be the Lord and Savior of the entire world! The titles *Savior* and *Lord* are quite provocative. One of the titles tends to ruffle our feathers mildly, and the other feels like we're getting our feathers plucked out! Some, when they hear that they need a Savior, are immediately offended because they believe they're sufficient in and of themselves. Others actually love the idea of a Savior! In fact, this is why we have superheroes. In the typical Superman moment, a building is on fire and the man of steel—with perfect teeth—flies in, rescues the woman in distress, and gets her to the ground safe and sound. The savior is praised and flies off to save someone else; the woman goes home, back to life as usual, thankful for Superman.

But Jesus isn't Superman. In Christianity, Jesus not only saves us, but remains *with us* and takes on the role of being our Lord for every moment of every day starting with the present moment and extending throughout all eternity. Lordship implies that someone else is in charge, leading, and in total control.

When the Bible uses the word *Lord* in reference to God, it means that he has ultimate authority. As soon as we hear the words *authority* or *lordship*, many of us become suspicious. This could be for any number of reasons. Parents, teachers, bosses, pastors, police officers, and so on all function as imperfect authorities in our lives. Some even go so far as to abuse their authority, heightening our distrust of anyone to whom we are held accountable. To say that Jesus is one's *Lord* is to define a key aspect of a person's relationship to him.

Jesus is not your homeboy. Jesus is not old news. Jesus is not the one who can be ignored for long. Jesus is Lord, and is preeminent in all things, including our thoughts, desires, and pursuits. The common temptation is to think that God gives certain commands simply because he is withholding something fun or pleasurable from us. But God is *good*. In fact, goodness cannot exist outside of or apart from Almighty God. He is *for* us. He is *with* us. He does not keep us *from* joy but gives us *full, real, complete, authentic* joy in and through following Jesus—both on the mountaintops and down in the valleys. Christian, it is imperative that you understand that Jesus being your *Lord* is not like a crooked cop—out to steal from, oppress, or forget about you! Jesus being Lord is part of the good news of the gospel!

### The Struggle Is Real

But as they say, "the struggle is real," and disobedience comes naturally to all of us. Sure, as Christians we have a new nature and we long to please our Lord (Ephesians 2:10). And yet, sin is still tempting, and sometimes we give in. Why is that? Because we are on our way to perfection, but we aren't there yet. That happens when we are glorified in heaven (Romans 8:30). So what happens when we disobey our Lord? Is our salvation in jeopardy? Should we expect him to drop a fireball on us? Does this mean that we were never saved to begin with? Those are definitely not easy questions. More than that, there are moments in the Bible where disobedience ends up costing people their lives. For example, Uzzah touches the ark, which was forbidden, and he dies instantly (2 Samuel 6:6–7). In the New Testament, there is a couple who lies about their giving to the church and they die immediately (Acts 5:1–10). Paul says that some people are sick and even have died as a result of taking Communion in an unworthy manner (1 Corinthians 11:29). What are we to make of moments like this in the Bible? Is this what we should expect to happen to us when we give in to temptation?

First, you must know that you cannot lose your salvation (John 6:39). You cannot earn it and you cannot lose it. You are not the author or perfecter of your faith. God is (Hebrews 12:2 NASB). Salvation is completely a gift from God (Ephesians 2:8–9), and we can trust him to save us completely. Second, these accounts in Scripture where people lose their lives are *descriptive* accounts of what happened to them and are not to be understood as *prescriptive* for all people and places. How do we know that? Because we've sinned against God and are alive right now! And yet, we ought to tread lightly, aware of how seriously God takes our sin. Sin is why the world is broken, why we suffer, and why Jesus had to face the horror of Calvary.

And yet, even with accounts like this in Scripture, we *still* find sin quite tempting! Resisting temptation, fleeing from sin, and walking in obedience are never popular, easy, or convenient. Put simply: obedience *costs.* As a disciple of Jesus, you're in a relationship in which both love and discipline are ongoing. When we sin, we are to do precisely what Jesus preached: We are to repent (Mark 1:14–15). Martin Luther was an integral player in the role of church history, as he helped usher in the Reformation by nailing the Ninety-five Theses to the door of the local Catholic church in Witten-berg, Germany. The first thesis states that "When our Lord and Master Jesus Christ said 'Repent,' he willed the entire life of believers to be one of repentance."[2] In other words, repentance is something that we continue to do. A healthy Christian is a repenting Christian. Beware of those who pro-fess to follow Jesus but never talk about their own need of him. Be wary of the preacher who says, "You need Jesus" more often than confessing his own need of Jesus. Walking in repentance doesn't mean that we go about covered in ashes, scourging ourselves, feeling miserable all the time. But it does mean that when we see sin in our lives, out of love for our Savior and obedience to our Lord, we repent and seek to go in the opposite direction.

The writer of Hebrews says,

> The Lord disciplines the one he loves, and he chastens everyone he accepts as his son. Endure hardship as disci-pline; God is treating you as his children. For what children are not disciplined by their father? . . . God disciplines us for our good, in order that we may share in his holiness.
>
> Hebrews 12:6–7, 10

In his grace, God lovingly disciplines his children with the aim of bringing his people back into right fellowship with himself through the conviction of sin, granting repentance, and extending mercy and forgiveness. But as the children of God, we still oftentimes find ourselves faced with what we would call a conflict of interest.

Paul describes the inner conflict that happens within all Christians. He says, "I do not understand what I do. For what I want to do I do not do, but what I hate I do" (Romans 7:15 NIV). He's frustrated, deeply grieved over his sin, and looks to Jesus for salvation, proclaiming that there is "no condemnation for those who are in Christ Jesus" (Romans 8:1). Let's look at two places in the Bible that put on display temptation, sin, and this inner struggle we all face as Christians. Probably the most famous act of disobedience recorded in the Bible comes to us in the story of Jonah, the rogue prophet. We'll look at Jonah's story, at King David, and then over to a few statements by Jesus.

## Comedy and Cruelty

The book of Jonah (written in the eighth century BC) is not only history but also a satirical comedy.[3] Jonah is the rogue prophet who fails every single assignment given to him. God says, "Go to Nineveh" (Jonah 1:2); Jonah goes "to Tarshish" (v. 3). God tells him to "call out against" the city (v. 2); Jonah falls asleep in a getaway boat (v. 5). As the storm is raging, in a moment of suicidal panic, Jonah asks to be "hurled into the sea," only to be swallowed by a great fish (vv. 12, 17)! Eventually, God is merciful to Jonah's enemies (3:10). What is Jonah's response to the outpouring of the grace of God? He's so angry that he finds himself thinking he'd be better off dead (4:1–9), because having to share his God with downright pagans was just too much to stomach.

Why such a dramatic, disobedient, passionate response to the call of God on his life? Why did running away seem like the thing to do? Why was Jonah so angry? Further, what does this have to do with you and me? More than we think. God still calls us to the difficult and seemingly impossible. You've probably heard the cliché that passes for actual Scripture: "God will never give you more than you can handle." But that's not what the Bible says. The reality is that God will not give you more than *he* can handle. Just look at the list of men and women mentioned above. All of them (and everyone since) have struggled immensely walking with God because sometimes obedience feels like too much to handle.

## Why Jonah Ran

Jonah's desire to run from the call of God makes perfect sense when we consider the historical context. There was a lot of bad blood between Israel and the Ninevites. Jonah's ancestors were victims of some of the cruelest acts in the history of the world, and those actions were carried out by the hands of the Ninevites.[4] For instance, they skinned their victims alive and then impaled their bodies on sharpened stakes, leaving them there to die in the sun. Oftentimes, parents were forced to watch their children being burned alive only to then face their own deaths. Victims were at times buried up to their necks in the sand and left to die of hunger or thirst, or to be devoured by wild animals. Their reputation was so fierce that on occasion entire cities would commit suicide rather than fall into the hands of the Ninevites. These are the people to whom God instructed Jonah to go, and Jonah went . . . in the opposite direction.

**When Running Away Feels Better**

After receiving his instructions to go to Nineveh, we read, "But Jonah rose to flee to Tarshish from the presence of the Lord. He went down to Joppa and found a ship going to Tarshish. So he paid the fare and went down into it, to go with them to Tarshish, away from the presence of the Lord" (1:3).

Jonah boards a ship that usually carried between thirty and fifty men, and heads toward Spain, which was about two thousand miles in the opposite direction from where he was instructed to go. After getting out to sea, Jonah thinks he's gotten away and falls asleep in the boat. Let's be honest, running away from God and going into blatant sin sometimes feels good. But only short-term. The pleasures of sin never last. And if you're God's child, he will pursue you passionately, bringing not condemnation (that went to Jesus at the cross!) but rather heavy conviction and discipline. You see, the Lord was not only interested in saving Nineveh, he was interested in saving Jonah from himself.

God then hurls a storm upon the sea, and the pagan fishing crew begins calling out to their gods, but none answer or deliver. They then wake Jonah from his sleep, and Jonah knows that the storm is indeed Yahweh's doing. Jonah confesses to the men that he's running from his God and insists that he should be hurled into the sea in order to appease the wrath of God. Much could be said about this, but suffice it to say that God never suggests suicide as the answer, but rather repentance. Someone else was destined to die for the sins of the world. Jonah is tossed into the sea, and it becomes calm again. The prophet bearing the message of God is now sinking, taken completely out of sight, doomed to die in his rebellion.

Then we read that "the Lord [YHWH = the God who saves] appointed a great fish to swallow up Jonah" (1:17). Certainly Jonah must've thought, "This is it. I'm doomed. I ran from God, and this is what I deserve." After all, what God owes a rebel is justice, not grace; death, not life; judgment, not rescue and redemption. But what looked like the death penalty for Jonah turned out to be his life preserver! The fish swallowing up Jonah was not the judgment of God! The fish was appointed by God to be Jonah's *rescuer*! Perhaps this was even in the minds of the early Christians when they decided to use a fish as a symbol of Christianity.

In the belly of the beast, Jonah prays. It is amazing sometimes how bad it has to get before we'll pray, isn't it? Jonah is no longer running from God, but is now turning to God. Interestingly enough, Jonah is not recorded as giving a specific confession of sin (hating his enemies, running from God, opting for suicide, etc.). He prays for deliverance from his circumstances, yet his heart is still murky. We know that his heart hasn't undergone a thorough change just yet because of how the book ends! After three days in the belly of the fish, God causes the fish to vomit Jonah up onto the seashore, and Jonah decides at this point he is going to be obedient to God and preach to the Ninevites. Reluctantly, Jonah preaches just one sentence to the people, they repent, and God grants them a reprieve.

The tragic comedy ends not with Jonah rejoicing in his own salvation, or the salvation of his enemies, but rather grumbling to God about the fact that the Ninevites should be despised, not saved. Jonah even begins talking about being better off dead than having to witness this audacious, totally scandalous act of God's grace. The writer of Jonah leaves the book open-ended for a reason. We are left to consider all of this and, much like a parable, evaluate our own lives. Have you been there? How would you feel if you were Jonah? How does the story of Jonah help you think about your life and how you approach obedience? When God puts the impossible before you, what are you going to do? How would you feel if God had mercy on your enemies? The reality is this: the heart of the disciple is exposed when God graces our enemies. Let's go back and press that repentance piece a bit, since Jonah didn't give us an explicit confession. What does a heartfelt confession of sin look and sound like? Let's look at King David.

## The Crooked King Made Straight

King David is known as the "man after [God's] own heart" (1 Samuel 13:14). As a boy, he killed the giant Goliath. He penned dozens of the psalms, led the nation as a king, and is even an ancestor of Jesus himself. In 2 Samuel 11, we read the infamous account of his episode with Bathsheba.

The nation of Israel is at war, and it is David's responsibility to lead the troops into battle. One particular evening, he opts out of his duties and decides to stay home and send the troops into battle on their own. While at home, he walks out onto his balcony, looks across the way, and sees a gorgeous woman, bathing nude on the roof of her house. The lust of the eyes grips him and he will not restrain himself. He *must* have her at all costs! He sends one of his men to find out who she is, and she turns out to be Bathsheba, Uriah's wife. Uriah is one of David's best men in the army. David has her brought to him. They enjoy each other's company, one thing leads to another, and David sleeps with her. A few weeks later, she sends word to David, saying, "I'm pregnant."

English theologian Isaac Barrow (1630–1677) said, "Sin is never at a stay; if we do not retreat from it, we shall advance in it, and the farther we go, the more we have to come back." David insists on going even further. He should confess his sins to God and to Uriah, telling him what they've done. But instead of dealing with his sin, he brings Uriah home, gets him drunk, and says, "Head on back to your wife." He hopes that Uriah, having been away from his wife while at war, and filled to the brim with wine, will naturally go home and sleep with Bathsheba. That way, when she announces her pregnancy, it will appear as though the child belongs to Uriah and not David. However, Uriah refuses to enjoy the company of his wife while the other soldiers are suffering. So David sends a letter to Joab, the commander, via the hand of Uriah, to have the men fall back when the battle is the fiercest so that Uriah will be killed, and David will be off the hook. After Uriah is dead, he marries Bathsheba and seeks to get on with his life. Just look at all the sin—all the lying, spinning, planning, deceiving, and ultimately the murder—that went into covering David's sin. This can't be excused because of all the good he's done for the nation and all his service to God. This is an absolute outrage and unjust on every level!

Solomon said, "He who covers his sins will not prosper" (Proverbs 28:13 NKJV). And that's exactly what happens. Because God disciplines those he loves (Deuteronomy 8:5; Hebrews 12:6), David doesn't get away with his sins. After a year goes by, God sends Nathan the prophet to confront David, and he is devastated. He knows what he has done is wrong and doesn't make excuses, but has a broken heart. He goes to God broken and repentant. He writes two psalms about his experiences of sin, disgrace, and the grace of God (Psalms 32 and 51).

In Psalm 32:1–5 David writes:

> Blessed is the one whose transgression is forgiven, whose sin is covered. Blessed is the man against whom the Lord counts no iniquity, and in whose spirit there is no deceit. For when I kept silent, my bones wasted away through my groaning all day long. For day and night your hand was heavy upon me; my strength was dried up as by the heat of summer. I acknowledged my sin to you, and I did not cover my iniquity; I said, "I will confess my transgressions to the Lord," and you forgave the iniquity of my sin.

The metaphor David uses here is applicable to anyone who claims to be a child of God and yet is living in rebellion to the will of God. David speaks of his bones, filled with poison, as an ongoing ache. That's what it felt like as he sought to keep all the sin, all the lies, all the deceit inside. He felt like he'd been working in the sun all day without a break, and the constant beating down of the heat had sapped all his strength and vitality. Why couldn't he just move on? Why was his conscience so bothered and his spirit so grieved? He belonged to God, and that's what unrepentant living actually feels like as a believer. If you're a new believer and are thinking of running off in rebellion, prepare for some aching bones and sapped strength. Because being a person after God's own heart is not about being perfect; it is about chasing what is perfect.

Look at how good, gracious, and forgiving David found his heavenly Father to be! The reality is that it all boils down to a raw confession of sin, coming out of hiding, blaming, and excuse making. Thomas à Kempis said, "I would rather *feel* compunction than know its definition."[5] David certainly felt it and experienced grace upon grace. When we fail in our obedience to our Lord, we must remember that he is not only our Lord, but our Savior, who extends forgiveness and pardon, restores us, and empowers us.

As referenced at the beginning of this chapter, the apostles were not sinless men who hovered above the earth, free of brushing against other fellow sinners, impervious to the grime and filth of the world. Just like you and me, they were made of flesh and bone, with real desires and temptations, too. No, that stuff didn't die out in the Old Testament. What did Jesus teach them and us about the nature of sin? Why is it so important that we flee from it with all of his strength working in us? Is sin really that big of a deal?

The answer is *yes*! Sin is rebellion against God and results in broken relationships with him, others, and even ourselves. Jesus said that when it comes to temptation to sin, we are to take extreme measures in dealing with it: "If your hand or foot causes you to stumble, cut it off and throw it away. It is better for you to enter life maimed or crippled than to have two hands or two feet and be thrown into eternal fire" (Matthew 18:8 NIV). It is clear here that Jesus is speaking in hyperbole, but his point stands. Sin is wicked, and those who would follow after him have determined to seek God, die to the temptations of the world, and find real joy in our King. This means that we are to go to war with sin.

Dear friends, it is not legalistic for God to call us to repentance and to remind us that we are not the God of the universe. That's grace. This is called waging war on what God hates, namely sin. Legalism is man's attempt to placate a false god with our own ideas of what holiness is supposed to look like. Legalism is just as dangerous as licentiousness. The legalistic person is the one who nominates himself to serve God's government as the local sheriff. But God never appointed that kind of nonsense. God isn't interested in his children competing with one another or keeping each other under a thumb. He wants his people to be free!

Seneca, a Roman statesman and philosopher of the first century, said it this way: "We see others' vices right before us, but we carry our own on our backs." Brothers and sisters, let us not give sight only to the sins of others while bearing our own "on our backs."[6] When a brother or sister sins, we are to lovingly confront them, pressing toward faith, repentance, and restoration. And not only that, may we bring our sins to the Savior.

Paul teaches, "Work out your own salvation with fear and trembling" (Philippians 2:12). But how are we to do it? How are we to live in obedience to God? He answers with "For it is *God* who works in you, both to will and to work for his good pleasure" (v. 13). Thus the way to go about killing sin and fleeing temptation is not found in your flesh, that is, in your own efforts. Rather, it is found in abiding in Jesus, looking to him, trusting in him, depending on him, and resting in him. How can we do this? God gives us the strength through the Holy Spirit. The power we have to resist sin comes not from us but from God.

Being *tempted* to sin is not *sinning*. Giving in to the temptation is sin. How do we avoid giving in to temptation? We are to "take every thought captive to make it obedient to Jesus" (2 Corinthians 10:5 NIV). This means that our minds are now in submission to Jesus in every way. What we think about, mull over, and dwell upon is of incredible importance for a disciple of Jesus. We are to have our minds renewed *continually* (Romans 12:1–2). The renewal of the mind for the Christian is not like the occasional holiday. We're called to live out of our identity as a new creation in Christ and to have our mind constantly renewed. The occasional Bible study and occasional prayer simply won't cut it.

We've been summoned to life with our King and his people, and this changes how we think about everything and everyone. We are to live in intentional community with other Christians and make it our aim to "encourage one another day after day, as long as it is still called 'Today,' so that none of you will be hardened by the deceitfulness of sin" (Hebrews 3:13 NASB) What exactly is going to sustain this battle against the flesh as we deal with the constant bombardment of lust, our insatiable appetites for more, our jockeying for position, our craving for the bigger, the better, the faster things of this world? What or who will be the center of all Christian discipleship? My friends, the only One who has the power to help us is Jesus. He sets us free to run straight toward the face of God.

> If we confess our sins, he is faithful and just to forgive us our sins and to cleanse us from all unrighteousness. If we say we have not sinned, we make him a liar, and his word is not in us.
>
> 1 John 1:9–10

### Questions to Consider

1. Are you prone to read the Bible moralistically? Do you look for the "good guys and bad guys"? How does it make you feel to know that Jesus is the ultimate hero in Scripture?

2. Where do you see Jesus asserting his lordship in your life? What is he calling you to repent of?

3. Maybe you're like Jonah and you're already running from God. What is keeping you from turning back? Read Psalm 32 and notice how David describes his joy that accompanies repentance.

# BAPTISM

*Cleansed*

> When you wash your face, remember your
> baptism.
>
> —Martin Luther

Baptism is the ancient and beautiful practice given by Jesus to the church. The how and the who of baptism have raised age-old debates. How is it to be done? Sprinkling, pouring, or immersion? Who can be baptized? Infants, children, or confessing adult believers? How many times should I be baptized? Regardless of where you are on these issues, baptism is one of the sacraments our Lord Jesus gave to the church. Like Communion, baptism uniquely belongs to the church. Another way to say it is that baptism is for those in God's family.

The great theologian J.I. Packer beautifully and succinctly says this:

Christian baptism, which has the form of a ceremonial washing (like John's pre-Christian baptism), is a sign from God that signifies inward cleansing and remission of sins (Acts 22:16; 1 Cor. 6:11; Eph. 5:25–27), Spirit-wrought regeneration and new life (Titus 3:5), and the abiding presence of the Holy Spirit as God's seal, testifying and guaranteeing that one will be kept safe in Christ forever (1 Cor. 12:13; Eph. 1:13–14). Baptism carries these meanings because first and fundamentally it signifies union with Christ in his death, burial, and resurrection (Rom. 6:3–7; Col. 2:11–12); and this union with Christ is the source of every element in our salvation (1 John 5:11–12). Receiving the sign in faith assures the persons baptized that God's gift of new life in Christ is freely given to them. At the same time, it commits them to live henceforth in a new way as committed disciples of Jesus. Baptism signifies a watershed point in a human life because it signifies a new-creational engrafting into Christ's risen life.[1]

Some understand baptism to be a symbol; others understand it to be more than a symbol. The complexities that swirl around the doctrine, subject, and practice of baptism are many. The aim in this chapter is not to delve into all the church history and nuances that go into various baptismal practices. I'd like to give a bit of the historical background of baptism and then point to just a few of the big ideas of what baptism certainly represents to *all* Christians regardless of what (if any) denomination they may belong to. A few years ago, *Christianity Today* posted an article that opened with "Most Christians view baptism either as the means of salvation and entry into the church or as a sign of Christ's redemptive work in the converted. In both cases, the new believer is considered wholly regenerated, and baptism seals this radical change."[2] Your local pastors, deacons, and church leaders should be able to fill you in on what your local church believes and practices regarding these issues and why or how they arrived at their conclusions.

## Old Testament

In the Pentateuch (the first five books of the Bible), we find the Law of God. In it, we see how Moses prescribes the use of water as a means of cleansing people who had become ceremonially defiled by coming in contact with a dead body, or someone with leprosy, contracting a disease, eating forbidden food, or emitting bodily fluids. Additionally, the Jewish people practiced circumcision, and baptism for Gentiles who wished to convert to Judaism. "The term *baptism* could indicate dipping, sprinkling, or immersion, but the Jewish custom was immersion."[3]

## New Testament

When we get to the New Testament, the first time we see baptism being practiced is with none other than John the Baptist. The gospel of Mark hits the ground running at an incredible pace with this passion-filled prophet who is preparing the way of the Lord Jesus by summoning the people to repent of their sin and be baptized. Mark does not mention the virgin birth or give the genealogy of Jesus as do Matthew and Luke.

John appeared, baptizing in the wilderness and proclaiming a baptism of repentance for the forgiveness of sins. And all the country of Judea and all Jerusalem were going out to him and were being baptized by him in the river Jordan, confessing their sins. Now John was clothed with camel's hair and wore a leather belt around his waist and ate locusts and wild honey. And he preached, saying, "After me comes he who is mightier than I, the strap of whose sandals I am not worthy to stoop down and untie. I have baptized you with water, but he will baptize you with the Holy Spirit."

Mark 1:4–8

The very next passage records *Jesus himself* being baptized.

In those days Jesus came from Nazareth of Galilee and was baptized by John in the Jordan. And when he came up out of the water, immediately he saw the heavens being torn open and the Spirit descending on him like a dove. And a voice came from heaven, "You are my beloved Son; with you I am well pleased."

vv. 9–11

Some might be tempted to think that maybe Jesus sinned before beginning his public ministry, and thus he, too, had to repent. However, Scripture firmly resists the idea that Jesus sinned (1 Peter 2:22; 2 Corinthians 5:21; Hebrews 4:15; 1 John 3:5). In fact, following his baptism, he goes straight to the desert and defeats Satan by resisting his temptations to sin.

So why was Jesus baptized? Matthew's gospel includes an interesting conversation recorded between Jesus and John the Baptist that helps us tremendously:

Then Jesus came from Galilee to the Jordan to John, to be baptized by him. John would have prevented him, saying, "I need to be baptized by you, and do you come to me?" But Jesus answered him, "Let it be so now, for thus it is fitting for us to fulfill all righteousness." Then he consented.

Matthew 3:13–15

Jesus' baptism speaks to his position of being our Great High Priest. The high priest in the Old Testament served in the temple, offering sacrifices for his own sins and the people's sins and serving as a mediator between God and Israel. The High Priest would have to be thirty years old (Numbers 4:1–3), washed with water (Exodus 29:1, 4; Leviticus 8:6; Numbers 8:7), anointed with oil (Exodus 29:7; Leviticus 8:12), and have a verbal confirmation or blessing said over him (Exodus 39:43; Numbers 6:22–27). Interestingly enough, that's what we see in Jesus' baptism. He is thirty years old, goes into the water, is anointed with the Holy Spirit, and the Father speaks his blessing over Jesus (Luke 3:21–23). Thus at his baptism, Jesus' public ministry began.

## Going Public

After rising triumphantly from the dead, Jesus gave what is commonly known as the Great Commission:

And Jesus came and said to them, "All authority in heaven and on earth has been given to me. Go therefore and make disciples of all nations, baptizing them in the name of the

115

Father and of the Son and of the Holy Spirit, teaching them to observe all that I have commanded you. And behold, I am with you always, to the end of the age."

Matthew 28:18–20

Notice here that baptism is a command given by Jesus to all who would call themselves his disciples. For someone to profess faith in Christ but refuse to be baptized would be walking in disobedience to his commandment. A question arises, "*When* should I get baptized?" The answer depends on the background knowledge that the believer already possesses. There are cases in the New Testament where we see someone baptized immediately upon confession of Jesus as their Lord (Acts 8:36). And yet, in early church history, a period of waiting was required. Church historian Justo González writes,

> In order to partake of communion one had to be baptized. In Acts we are told that people were baptized as soon as they were converted. This was feasible in the early Christian community, where most converts came from Judaism or had been influenced by it, and thus had a basic understanding of the meaning of Christian life and proclamation. But, as the Church became increasingly Gentile, it was necessary to require a period of preparation, trial, and instruction prior to baptism. This was the "catechumenate," which, by the beginning of the third century, lasted three years. During that time, catechumens received instruction on Christian doctrine, and were to give signs in their daily lives of the depth of their conviction. Finally, shortly before being baptized,

they were examined and added to the list of those to be baptized.[4]

While it can be done immediately, many Christians choose to wait for a short period of time, meet with their pastors, and really understand what it means to follow Jesus and to be baptized before proceeding. If you are a Christian and haven't been baptized, make it a priority to meet with your pastor to talk about it.

The apostles were instructed to baptize disciples in the name of the Father, Son, and Holy Spirit. It is interesting to see the Trinity mentioned here. "We should notice that the word *name* is singular; Jesus does not say that his followers should baptize in the 'names' of Father, Son, and Holy Spirit, but in the 'name' of these three. It points to the fact that they are in some sense one."[5] For a Christian, being baptized in the name of the triune God is to publicly proclaim one's relationship with the Father, Son, and Holy Spirit. The Trinity is lovingly involved in the creating, saving, and rearing of the children of God. "God has sent the Spirit of his Son into our hearts, crying, 'Abba! Father!'" (Galatians 4:6). Baptism signifies that there has been a break with our former way of life and we are now living by, in, and to Christ. Since it is public, "Baptism was to conversion something like what the engagement ring is to many engaged couples in modern Western society; the official, public declaration of the commitment."[6] As baptism is an event that takes place usually in church services in which the members gather, it serves as a means of identifying with Christ and his people.

**Washing of Sins**

Baptism not only speaks to being in communion with the triune God but also addresses the fact that we are "cleansed" before God. "Baptism is a means of appropriating the benefits of Christ's saving work (*wash your sins away*) and receiving the promised forgiveness of sins. The image of washing in 1 Corinthians 6:11; Ephesians 5:26; Titus 3:5; and Hebrews 10:22 is also probably linked to baptism."[7] Ananias said to Paul upon his conversion, "And now what are you waiting for? Get up, be baptized and wash your sins away, calling on his name" (Acts 22:16 NIV).

*Cleansed?* What an absolutely beautiful gift of God! "Outward washing with water expresses the cleansing from sin that is proclaimed in the gospel and received by faith sacramentally in baptism."[8] Jesus tells the disciples they are clean (John 15:3). John tells the early church, "If we confess our sins, he is faithful and just to forgive us our sins and to *cleanse* us from all unrighteousness" (1 John 1:9). Baptism points to our cleanliness before God. Martin Luther reportedly said, "When you wash your face, remember your baptism." This is a helpful practice that goes with you every day of your life. Every time you wash your face or hop in the shower, remember, *God has made me clean.*


**Death, Burial, and Resurrection Depicted**

A Christian baptism is an absolutely beautiful demonstration of the core of the gospel message! Look at what Paul writes to the Corinthian church:

> For I delivered to you as of first importance what I also
> received: that Christ died for our sins in accordance with
> the Scriptures, that he was buried, that he was raised on
> the third day in accordance with the Scriptures.
>
> 1 Corinthians 15:3–4

When someone goes under the water, they are identifying with Jesus in his death and burial (Romans 6:4; Colossians 2:12). Coming back out of the water is identifying with his resurrection.

## Womb and the Tomb

There is a saying from the early church that can serve to help us better understand what water baptism *is* and what it *represents*. Sofia Cavalletti, a woman who lived in Rome and worked with young children on their spiritual formation, writes in her book *Living Liturgy: Elementary Reflections*:

> The catechumens [Christian converts awaiting baptism] went down into the baptismal pool, which was considered both the tomb of the old person and the motherly womb of the church, which gave new birth to the new person. Going into the pool was like going down into the tomb, and coming up out of the pool was the return to a new life, the life of the risen Christ.[9]

So, if you walk into your church and you see the baptismal font, think to yourself, *from death to life*. You see, as you're baptized, you're in a sense reaching back in time to hold the

119

hands of the saints who have gone before us, and remembering the stark reality that our old lives with all of our sin and folly are buried in the tomb, and by the grace of God, we emerge to live new lives from the womb as the people of God.

The baptismal font is the tomb and the womb.

### QUESTIONS TO CONSIDER

1. Have you been baptized? If so, take a moment to reflect on that experience.

2. If you haven't been baptized, why not? Are you preparing to do so?

3. One very important element of baptism is the image of being *cleansed* entirely. Do you see yourself as cleansed of all sin?

# CHURCH MEMBERSHIP

Now you are the body of Christ, and each one
of you is a part of it.

—1 Corinthians 12:27 NIV

*Church membership.* As soon as you read those two words, you
may cringe or have questions racing through your head: *What
on earth does it even mean? What is the point of church membership? Aren't these just empty words? After becoming a Christian,
does the Bible say I have to actually join a local church? Doesn't
the church become less powerful when it organizes? Shouldn't
it remain "organic"? Can't I just have Jesus and not the church?
What if I like to go from church to church in my community and
not commit to just one? Besides, I've already become a Christian,
which makes me the weird one in my family, among friends, and
in my workplace. Could you come up with anything more lame
than becoming a church member?* These are the kinds of questions that we will be diving into in this chapter.

## What Is Church Membership?

Before getting into the how's and why's of church membership, we should define what it is up front.

Jonathan Leeman wrote a book on the subject and says,

> Church membership is a formal relationship between a
> church and a Christian characterized by the church's affir-
> mation and oversight of a Christian's discipleship and the
> Christian's submission to living out his or her discipleship
> in the care of the church.[1]

Thus, membership is a two-way covenant, or commitment, between the individual and the church. This definition is helpful for so many reasons. Let's start with the shepherds.

## Elders: Committed to Shepherding the Flock

Look at how Paul boldly challenges the elders in Ephesus: "Pay careful attention to yourselves and to all the flock, in which the Holy Spirit has made you overseers, to care for the church of God, which he obtained with his own blood" (Acts 20:27–28).

Paul reminds the elders that they are shepherds and that the people entrusted to their care are of infinite value. If you're a new Christian, be reminded again that Jesus gave his life for you and has "obtained" you, meaning that you are his very own. Next, remember that it is Jesus who saves, not the church. It was Jesus who shed his blood for you, not the local leaders. Paul is charging the leaders "to care for the church of God."

This means they are to lovingly lead, guide, protect, and feed the sheep with incredible diligence. The Bible does not mince words about *how* God wants his sheep cared for. Passages such as Ezekiel 34:1–10 will show you what kind of shepherds to avoid. They're the lazy ones who use the sheep, abuse the sheep, and neglect the sheep. The sheep are used as a means to their own selfish ends. God strongly rebukes them for taking this posture and attitude toward God and his people. The requirements that an elder in the local church ought to fulfill are clearly spelled out in 1 Timothy 3:1–7 and Titus 1:5–9. And here's how the apostle Peter told the elders to go about caring for the church:

> So I exhort the elders among you, as a fellow elder and a witness of the sufferings of Christ, as well as a partaker in the glory that is going to be revealed: shepherd the flock of God that is among you, exercising oversight, not under compulsion, but willingly, as God would have you; not for shameful gain, but eagerly; not domineering over those in your charge, but being examples to the flock. And when the chief Shepherd appears, you will receive the unfading crown of glory.
>
> 1 Peter 5:1–4

Notice how the shepherds are to go about caring for the flock in light of the imminent return of the Chief Shepherd, the Lord Jesus. As you consider becoming a member of the church, look into and explore the kinds of pastors that are in place. Can you tell if they're domineering or being good examples? The shepherds in the church are under the Chief

Shepherd, the Lord Jesus. This means that shepherds are also sheep, who get to serve as under-shepherds.

It is the responsibility of the elders to see to it that church members are equipped to do the work of the ministry (Ephesians 4:11–13). They are to serve the members of the church by praying regularly for them, as seen repeatedly in Paul's letters, and by being available to anoint with oil and pray for those who are sick (James 5:14). Shepherds are to care for members by preaching, teaching, and providing wisdom, insight, and direction from the entire counsel of the Word of God (Acts 20:27–28; 1 Timothy 5:17). Elders are to guard the members from false teachers (Acts 20:29–31). Additionally, elders are to carry out the practice of church discipline, which will be discussed below (Matthew 18:15–20; 1 Corinthians 5; Galatians 6:1).[2]

## Membership Helps the Shepherds

Membership helps keep the relationships clear, defining who will be responsible to and for whom. The writer of the epistle to the Hebrews has some very sobering words for both members of the church and leaders: "Obey your leaders and submit to them, for they are keeping watch over your souls, as those who will have to give an account" (13:17). Having a formal membership process in place is necessary in order to obey this command. Without actually identifying with the local body and coming under qualified, identifiable leadership, the believer is left without one who is to be *looking after her soul*. Your soul was worth Jesus' shedding his blood to redeem. It only stands to reason that once you know this and believe it, you find a place where you can be looked after in a biblical way. Furthermore, how is a pastor expected to answer for a soul that has never identified with the body? If you're in a heavily churched area, does that mean all the pastors are responsible for all the professing Christians? What about major doctrinal disagreements? Certainly, having established church membership helps ground the relationship and communicates to the leader, "Here, specifically, is who you are responsible to look after and care for."

## Willing to Be Led

At the end of the day, being a member of a church is voluntarily coming under qualified leadership. It is taking the risk to have faith and trust in someone else to lead you spiritually. This does not negate the role of the Holy Spirit in your life in any way. In fact, this seems to be the preferred means by which he leads his people. As you will experience time and again, all leaders are flawed, sinful, and make mistakes. There is no such thing as a perfect leader. Even in the New Testament, we see the apostle Paul having to correct the apostle Peter. Outside of Jesus, no one is infallible.

Submitting to authority didn't sound appealing to believers in the first century, and it most certainly doesn't sound thrilling today, does it? And yet, church membership is actually a beautiful, mature, God-honoring privilege that you get to participate in as a devoted disciple of Jesus. As discussed earlier in the book, Jesus will make demands of us that simply don't square with our flesh. "Love your enemies" (Luke 6:35), for example. The road of discipleship is one long exhaling death to self and one gigantic inhaling living to Christ. Church membership is a part of this process.

As Christians, we know that Jesus does not seek to squash our joy. In fact, he's committed to our highest joy! This includes becoming a member of the local church. I know this still must sound unnecessary to some. With all that makes life so unbelievably busy these days, why in the world would someone want to become a member of a church and covenant with all of these people to do all of these things? Well, as a Christian, you already know the answer—with life as crazy as it is, the only thing more crazy would be to forego the amazing opportunity given to you in becoming a member of the church! Sure, joining a church won't make sense to your friends who aren't Christians. "You're going to give your time and effort to all of that? Isn't going to church once in a while good enough?" But they don't understand that you're a part of a different kingdom; you have a different worldview; your values have changed so much that what doesn't make sense to them makes total sense to you. Being a Christian isn't an idea or a hobby or small set of beliefs. Following Jesus is life.

When you became a Christian, you became a member of the body of Christ, or the universal church. This church is made up of all Christians everywhere. By becoming a member of a local body of Christ, you're agreeing with that specific church's beliefs and affirming the local leadership, mission, and vision of the church. This doesn't mean you can't disagree or have questions about certain things. If you do, go to your leaders and respectfully ask for help.

If you do find that you cannot agree with the beliefs or leadership, then it would be best to put becoming a member of that church on hold as you seek answers or simply move on to another church body.

As you ask questions or move on to another church, there are a few things that need to be more important than savvy logos and good coffee. Look for a church that exalts Jesus, submits to the Word of God, and has an emphasis on making disciples and engaging those who are far from Christ with the good news of the gospel. This can be quite challenging, but it is essential to your growth in Christ. So whatever you do—don't let up! Pursue the body of Christ like you need her . . . because you do. And, believe it or not, the body needs you, too.

As a member, you're agreeing to actively, regularly, consistently participate in the life of the body. You are not just an occasional attender who shows up from time to time and consumes whatever the church has to offer. No! You're a *member*! These people are *your* people! Becoming a member of a church is a strong step toward real biblical maturity. As a child, it was natural to take whatever you wanted and not give back or seek to contribute to the needs around you. Why? Because you were a child. You were immature.

As an active member of your church, you're not out to critique, criticize, or consume the church. You're out to bring life, light, and joy, and to serve her, because those people aren't just "those people" anymore. They become "my people." You no longer want to take, you want to give. You no longer want to just consume, you want to contribute. You want to treat church not as an option but as a *priority*.

Becoming a member of a church is a beautiful thing! The people whom you encounter over the years grow closer and closer to you. Some of them actually become closer to you than your own biological family! You'll enjoy deeper, more meaningful conversations and relationships with those people than with anyone else on the earth. We'll talk about this in our next chapter on community.

## Responding to Common Objections

In the introduction to this chapter, I listed some objections to becoming a member of a church. Some will say there is no explicit command in the Bible to sign a membership covenant. And it's true, the Bible does not say specifically that we should join a church. It also doesn't tell us exactly what the Sunday liturgy should be, how many worship services should be held each week, or any other number of things that are left to our judgment. But we must proceed. Growing in your relationship with God will be next to impossible outside of being formally committed to the local church.

Truly, Jesus gave his life for his people and expects them to dwell together. More than that, the apostle Paul uses the body metaphor as he reminds us that we are members of one another and that one member cannot say to another, "I have no need of you" (1 Corinthians 12:20–21). The reality is that the body needs you and you need the body in order to grow up strong in the faith. Church membership aids in fulfilling these scriptural expectations of those who claim to know and follow Jesus.

Others struggle with the idea of a church "organizing" itself. Some are tempted to think that somehow a disorganized faith is biblical. However, that couldn't be further from the case! For example, in Acts we find elders and deacons praying and discerning who should be doing what in order to care for the day-to-day needs of the people (Acts 6). More than that, at Pentecost, Peter preached and 3,000 people were added in a single day. How do we know that? Because this living organism was organized! They were actually keeping count. Why? Because those are people Jesus died for and redeemed. They were taking Jesus and the salvation he extends to sinners very seriously. Organization is not the enemy of being "organic." Organization does not quench the work of the Holy Spirit. Organization shows thoughtfulness, care, structure, and intentionality. Organizing shows that there is a plan and purpose to the gathering of the body. This is what love looks like.

Just as a good parent has a plan for their child's well-being, so good church leadership has a plan for the people Jesus died to redeem. If you want to do a case study, consider 1 Timothy 5:3–16, where we see how they were going about caring for widows in the church. This plan communicates thoughtfulness, intentionality, and above all, *love.*

Others object to becoming a member of a local church in favor of serving the body in a more indirect, generic sense. Read what Steve Timmis and Tim Chester write in their book *Total Church*:

Some people take a fluid view of church in the name of the universal church. They go to a conference, join a short-term team, participate in a parachurch organization, claiming that all these constitute their commitment to the church. There may be some validity in calling these things church in some sense. But they are not a substitute for the community that the New Testament presupposes is the context of the Christian life. It is easy to love the church in the abstract or to love people short-term. But we are called to love people as we share our lives with them. This is the pathway to Christian growth and holiness. Commitment to the people of God is expressed through commitment to specific congregations.[3]

## Commit to Just One Church Family

This answer applies to those who would ask, "What if I like to go from church to church in my community and not commit to just one?" There's that word *commit*. Commitment sounds boring, predictable, and lacking a certain excitement that we've come to think we're entitled to. We all admire the couple celebrating their sixtieth wedding anniversary; we read nostalgic stories about friendships that have weathered the greatest of trials; we watch movies in awe of people overcoming their greatest fears. But showing up at a party, reading a book, or watching a movie is entirely different from experiencing these things yourself. These are some praiseworthy accomplishments. But to actually pursue something of value is another thing altogether.

Consider that the church does not exist for the mere entertainment of the masses. The church exists in order to make

God's image-bearers whole in Jesus Christ. This is time-consuming, frustrating, and altogether beautiful. Over the years, I have observed just how consumer-oriented many folks are in their understanding of church here in the West. "I go here for the music. I go there for the preaching. I go across town because they've got a great kids' program. I go to my friend's church for the coffee."

There are also many churches that actually play into this kind of immaturity, offering gimmicks instead of grace. This isn't the place to go into a full-blown discussion on church architecture and programs. However, as you look to join a church, don't select one that you know is going to be content to let you show little to no growth in your faith. Join the church that is going to stretch you, challenge you, and truly encourage you in your walk with Jesus.

## Church Discipline: Restorative, Not Punitive

The idea of church discipline might sound completely crazy to you for any number of reasons, and I totally understand that. But know the idea of church discipline didn't originate with the church, but proceeded from the mouth of Jesus himself. In Matthew 18, Jesus lays out why and how to deal with conflict in the church. He explains how to approach the one in sin with the aim of "winning your brother" back. We see different cases of church discipline being employed throughout the New Testament. The heart behind church discipline, or any discipline, matters tremendously! If church discipline is found to be punitive rather than restorative, things go very, very badly. That is to say that if the process is not clear and if communication isn't thorough and seasoned with incredible grace, people will feel used and abused and will suffer great harm.

Spiritual abuse in the name of "church discipline" is something that is a real problem. For those who have experienced this, the desire to join another body, to trust the leaders, to invest one's time and treasures, is no longer easy or even desirable. The wounded saint often retreats into seclusion in order to protect himself from more pain. As you seek to join a church, ask the local leadership what their stance is on church discipline and how they go about doing it. If they have no plan for what to do with saints who sin, then they clearly need to go back and look closely at the New Testament.

The aim of church discipline is to be *restorative* in nature. In Galatians 6:1, Paul gives us explicit instructions on the *heart* that is to accompany the work of church discipline: "If any of you is caught in sin, let those of you who are spiritual seek to restore him, lest you too be tempted." The idea behind being "caught" here is different than what many naturally think. That is, Paul has not asked those who are strong in the faith to play the role of religious cops, keeping an eye out, policing the homes of the people, hoping to *catch* somebody in sin and bust them, embarrass them, and write them up or write them off. Rather, the emphasis is on the idea of an animal being *caught* in a trap: a Christian caught in and ensnared by the deceitfulness of sin. When that happens—not if, but *when* that happens—the church has the *responsibility* to respond gently and quickly with grace and truth with the intention of seeing that wayward sheep restored fully.

The reason Jesus gave discipline to the church is that as the head of the church, Jesus cares deeply about each member progressing in joyful holiness. The writer of Hebrews tells us that God "disciplines the one he loves" (Hebrews 12:5–6). This motive should fill the hearts of those doing the discipline. Paul admonishes all Christians, "Let all that you do be done in love" (1 Corinthians 16:14). If leaders serve the church without love, the church is bound to be just another bland, boring, religious club dominated by fear, shame, and self-righteousness.

At the end of the day, a member undergoing church discipline should be able to say, "This is painful, but I feel loved and can see the Holy Spirit working in my life and making me more like Jesus." Bottom line: If church discipline is done poorly, it's highly unlikely someone will recover from both the sin they committed and the poor treatment by those who are responsible for seeing the wayward sheep restored. However, when it is done well, and the sheep are restored, they'll never stop saying thank you to those who loved them enough to give them both grace and truth and walk it out with them.

### Questions to Consider

1. Does your church have a membership process in place?
2. Are you a member of a local church?
3. If you're on the fence about becoming a member, make it a priority to sit down with your pastor and talk about it.

# LIFE IN THE CHURCH COMMUNITY

> I didn't go to religion to make me happy. I always knew a bottle of Port would do that. If you want religion to make you feel really comfortable, I certainly don't recommend Christianity.
>
> —C. S. Lewis, *God in the Dock*

*Community* is one of those words that buzz around day after day in the local church. Why? Well, it is quite simple: Community is vitally important, and it has been since the very beginning. Not the beginning of the church, but even before that! Before the beginning of the beginning! God himself is in community as a Trinity and has made us in his image to be in community, both with himself and with others. A high premium should be placed on community in every local church. Jesus refers to the church as his bride, and just like a good husband, Jesus always introduces those he saves to his bride. God did not design salvation to be experienced alone and in isolation. No! He saves a *people* to himself and for himself and desires that they live in community—loving one another, serving one another, and exalting Jesus together in all things. These people come from every race, tribe, tongue, people group, socioeconomic background, political party, and so forth. The church is as diverse as the world itself because God is interested in all peoples.

## Types of Community

Different churches promote community in different ways. In a small church, the entire congregation may be able to interact and get to know one another in an up-close, personal way. Community will be created in Sunday services, prayer meetings, and social gatherings after church services or throughout the week.

Other churches are too big for the entire congregation to interact on a deeper level. These churches often provide opportunities for smaller groups of people to get together and form communities. These groups are often somewhere between six and twenty people who gather weekly as a Sunday school class or at someone's home for prayer, Bible study, and fellowship. They may be called life groups, small groups, community groups, or something to this effect. Oftentimes churches will take the content that is being taught on Sunday mornings and develop that further to be discussed in groups where people can ask questions and go a little deeper together.

Groups may be organized around an age group or other commonalities, such as college-age groups, singles' groups, or women's groups. Groups may meet in homes, dorms, condos, coffee shops, or even parks. One thing to ask about as you join a local church is whether they have these types of groups, and are they open to new members? Do they allow unbelievers to join the discussion? Do they allow participants to come and go as they please? Then there are other practical questions to ask, such as how often the group meets and whether the group serves the community in some way.

That's a very condensed introduction to the philosophy of community. At the end of this chapter, I have included several books to consult on the topic.

Now I want to return to the *relational* heart behind community.

### The Gift of Community

Theologians tend to talk about grace in two basic categories: common grace and special grace. Special grace speaks to the work of God to bring about salvation to his people. Common graces are those gifts from God that everyone has the capacity to enjoy: a sunrise or sunset, a shared meal with family or friends, the beauty of nature around us. The ability to enjoy community with others falls into the common grace category. One does not have to be a Christian in order to reap the benefits of community. However, *as Christians*, we know that God is the great Giver of all good and perfect gifts (James 1:17). *Everything* we enjoy is charged with incredible meaning because we know *who* these gifts proceed from, and thus every experience becomes an opportunity to worship.

A filet and glass of wine can be enjoyed to the glory of God not just because it tastes wonderful, but because we know the God who gives us this pleasure. A sunset's beauty is intensified knowing the Artist behind it all! And community, savoring life together, really being there for one another, celebrating the wins, mourning the losses—all with Jesus in the center—becomes completely invaluable to believers. As a child of God, you get to enjoy sharing life with those who know that they're saved by the same grace that you are. They walk with the same Jesus you walk with. They're filled with the same Holy Spirit you're filled with. Their Abba Father is the same Abba you talk with every day.

But this doesn't mean Christian community is without significant problems. It has been challenging since the beginning of the church, as you can tell through reading almost any of the letters in the New Testament. Christians don't always get along and see eye to eye. Even the apostles had moments where they ended up going their separate ways, though that is the exception and not the norm. Community can be tough. My hope in this book has been to show you some of the real stuff that comes with being a believer. The worst thing that can happen to someone is to be told, "Now that you've met Jesus, life is going to be super-easy for you from this day forward." Yeah, right. That never happens. In fact, following Jesus can make life more complicated than it was before. Why? You're dealing with sin and grace and truth and repentance and forgiveness and everything that comes with applying the gospel in community.

## Twenty-First-Century Community

The culture in which we live today, with its focus on radical individualism, is a formidable obstacle to authentic Christian community. Current philosophy, technology, and the day-to-day rhythm of life all compete against community. Much of our radical Western individualism can be traced to the eighteenth century, the dawn of the Industrial Revolution, the Age of Enlightenment, and the famous line by Rene Descartes, *"Cogito ergo sum,"* "I think, therefore I am." At this point in Western history, people have felt as though they had public permission to give in to what had always lurked within the human heart: the temptation to withdraw from God and community in the name of *self*.

And now, in the age of the avatar, we find ourselves with the power to create an online profile, an image, a persona, an identity. We control what we look like and selectively post only the highlight reels of our lives for others to "like." We all know that social media doesn't tell the whole story about the lives we see every day on our screens, but it still sinks into our minds in some profound ways. There are many sociopsychological effects that social media is having on the world today. We are more connected than we've ever been and yet more lonely, isolated, and insecure than ever before. As we scroll through all of our electronic friends' photos and status updates, we're tempted to believe that everyone else in the world is enjoying life, having amazing meals and experiences, and we're just sitting here on the couch—bored, lame, and uninteresting. And yet, the reality is that those people are just as lonely. This isn't an anti–social media rant. It's stating the facts in light of the gospel.

The day-to-day rhythms of our lives really muddy the waters when it comes to placing value on Christian community. We get up, go to work or school, fight traffic, pull in the garage, close the door, and enter our homes. We've got soccer practice, homework, games, yard work, and the list goes on and on. It seems like there's hardly enough time to get our regular routines done, much less go "varsity" with all that Christian community stuff. We could come up with endless reasons why Christian community doesn't need to be a priority in our lives. But let's just call it what it is: We're busy, easily offended, and selfish. Bearing one another's burdens, speaking the truth in love, and being available to others are all ways in which we die to ourselves and live for the glory of God and joy of the church.

The writer of Hebrews says,

> And let us consider how we may spur one another on toward love and good deeds, not giving up meeting together, as some are in the habit of doing, but encouraging one another—and all the more as you see the Day approaching.
>
> 10:24–25 NIV

This is an invitation to dive into and enjoy what God intends his people to enjoy, namely himself among themselves. It also gives us the opportunity to put the gospel on display in ways that will certainly cause heads to turn.

## Realistic Expectations

In order to stay grounded over the long haul of the Christian journey, every Christian must remember that nobody is perfect; none of their fellow brothers and sisters in the faith has "arrived" just yet. Like those going through puberty, all Christians are in the awkward stage of discipleship on our way to glory and being made perfect (Romans 8:30). But being on your way to being made perfect and actually being perfect in the present tense are two drastically different things. If you've ever met a Christian, you'll know pretty early on in the relationship precisely *why* they are in need of a Savior. Christians are the ones in need of saving, healing, forgiveness, and redemption. Christians are the ones who don't always get it right, can be selfish, rude, inconsistent, and often hypocritical. They are also the ones who trust God to be gracious to them based on what they know of Jesus and what they see Jesus extending to them in the gospel.

To join the Christian community is to join up with the people who acknowledge that they are responsible for the most evil event in the history of the world—namely, the death of the only Son of God. These are the people who have come to terms with the fact that they have fallen short, broken every commandment, and simply don't possess the will or the strength to save their own souls. But they believe that Jesus can save them, does save them, and has saved them! When one becomes a Christian and joins a local church community, he should expect sin and repentance, rebellion and grace, pain and healing to be present. That's what we see with Jesus in the Gospels, and the apostles in the churches. The reality is that Jesus' people, no matter how hard we try, can be a messy lot. Fights break out; churches split.

With this kind of reputation, the risk to trust and enter into community is high.

Yet hear me: Delving into isolation or settling for just a surface-level relationship with the church is, in fact, a higher risk. Why? Because taking that route is to assert that you know better than Jesus, thus making his command not to neglect meeting together (Hebrews 10:25) null and void. Jesus is convinced that you not only need the Holy Spirit but you also need *his people*. No, the people don't save you, but the people play a vital role in your sanctification. *To treat the church as optional is to miss the heart of the gospel by a mile.* Paul says, "Christ loved the church and gave himself up for her" (Ephesians 5:25). God doesn't have back-up plans. He makes one plan and finishes it. The church is God's plan A. You may not like that or agree with that; you may even think that his plan is a bad idea. When you feel that way, fret not. Every Christian has had a problem in the church at some point. Hear this again: The church is not something optional for the Christian. The church is essential. Why? Because as a Christian, you must give your life *to* the very thing Jesus gave his life *for*: the church, God's people.

## We Are a Thoroughly "Confessing" Community

As a community gathered around Jesus, we confess. The word *confess* means "to acknowledge a fact publicly." To be a Christian is to be able to confess from the heart two things: the Apostles' Creed (because it covers the basic beliefs of the church) and our sins to one another. The Apostles' Creed was not written by the apostles, but rather summarizes the core nonnegotiable tenants of what they taught. Penned in approximately AD 390, it beautifully captures what we believe and confess as Christians:

> I believe in God, the Father Almighty, the Maker of heaven and earth, and in Jesus Christ, His only Son, our Lord: Who was conceived by the Holy Ghost, born of the virgin Mary, suffered under Pontius Pilate, was crucified, dead, and buried. He descended into hell. The third day He arose again from the dead; He ascended into heaven, and sitteth on the right hand of God the Father Almighty; from thence he shall come to judge the quick and the dead. I believe in the Holy Ghost; the holy Christian church; the communion of saints; the forgiveness of sins; the resurrection of the body; and the life everlasting. Amen.[1]

Because we confess the Apostles' Creed and know that our salvation is secure in Jesus, we can confess our sins to one another. Jesus expects his followers to be up-front with each other, not passive-aggressive folks who expect others to read our minds. This doesn't mean we have to be forward or harsh. But it does mean that we take responsibility for our relationships. Thus, Jesus says:

> If your brother or sister sins, go and point out their fault, just between the two of you. If they listen to you, you have won them over. But if they will not listen, take one or two others along, so that "every matter may be established by the testimony of two or three witnesses." If they still refuse to listen, tell it to the church; and if they refuse to listen

even to the church, treat them as you would a pagan or a
tax collector.

Matthew 18:15–17

The aim of pointing out sin is to "win" the person over. In
Christian community, the win is never just seeking to win
an argument; it is to win a person. James admonishes us to
"confess your sins to one another and pray for one another,
that you may be healed" (5:16). There is healing in confession
of sin. In fact, the only way to walk in the light and lift the
weight of a conscience ridden by unrepentant sin is to confess
that sin to other faithful, mature believers in your community
who can apply the gospel to you and help you walk away from
it. Notice that I said, "faithful, mature believers." You need to
be careful that you don't confess your sin to someone who
is known to be a gossip or someone who cannot help you.
Paul tells the Christians in Rome to "welcome one another"
(Romans 15:7), and the community in Colossae, "Let the
word of Christ dwell in you richly, teaching and admonish-
ing one another in all wisdom, singing psalms and hymns
and spiritual songs, with thankfulness in your hearts to God"
(Colossians 3:16). Just looking at a few of these verses, we
can get an idea of what the climate of the community should
look and feel like.

## When It All Gets Real

Take some time to look at the epistle to the Romans. After
spending eleven chapters laying out the creation of the

world, the fall of mankind, the redemption given to believers through Jesus, our identity in Christ through the gospel and pointing toward future glory, Paul takes all of this and applies it horizontally, in *community*. This should practically and profoundly impact your community. Read his words:

> For as in one body we have many members, and the members do not all have the same function, so we, though many, are one body in Christ, and individually members one of another. Love one another with brotherly affection. Outdo one another in showing honor. Contribute to the needs of the saints and seek to show hospitality. Rejoice with those who rejoice, weep with those who weep. Live in harmony with one another. Do not be haughty, but associate with the lowly. Never be wise in your own sight. Repay no one evil for evil, but give thought to do what is honorable in the sight of all. If possible, so far as it depends on you, live peaceably with all.
>
> Romans 12:4–5, 10, 13, 15–18

This is what a kingdom-minded community looks like! They're not competing with each other, except in coming up with ways to outdo one another in showing honor! Their needs are being met. It is a relationally intelligent community of folks who know that when a friend succeeds it's time to throw a party. When a sudden tragedy befalls a family, a marriage starts coming apart at the seams, someone loses their job, or a community member has any other heartrending experience, the believers don't tell the one suffering to "let go and let God" and move on. No! They enter not with all the answers, but with tears. This is an understanding community. This is a peaceable community. This is a repentant community. This is a loving community. This is an encouraging community. This is Jesus' community.

## Resources on Community

Dodson, Jonathan K., and Brad Watson. *Called Together: A Guide to Forming Missional Communities.* GCD Books, 2014.

House, Brad. *Community: Taking Your Small Group Off of Life Support.* Wheaton, IL: Crossway, 2011.

McNeal, Reggie. *Missional Communities: The Rise of the Post Congregational Church.* San Francisco: Jossey-Bass, 2011.

Timmis, Steve. *Everyday Church: Gospel Communities on Mission.* Wheaton, IL: Crossway, 2012.

Vanderstelt, Jeff. *Saturate: Being Disciples of Jesus in the Everyday Stuff.* Wheaton, IL: Crossway, 2015.

### QUESTIONS TO CONSIDER

1. Have you ever considered that God himself, the Trinity, is a community? How does this impact how you think of him and those around you?

2. Do you tend to see the call to community as a burden or a blessing?

3. What are some obstacles in your life that are hindering you from dwelling in a Christ-centered community?

4. Look at those verses in Romans 12 again. Think about, envision, and pray for your community to follow what Paul lays out here.

# WHAT ABOUT MY MONEY?

> God wants your heart. He isn't looking just
> for donors for His kingdom, those who stand
> outside the cause and dispassionately consider
> acts of philanthropy. He's looking for disciples
> who are immersed in the causes they give to.
> He wants people who are so filled with a vi-
> sion for eternity that they wouldn't dream of
> not investing their money, time, and prayers
> where they will matter most.
>
> —Randy Alcorn, *The Treasure Principle*

If the previous several chapters haven't shown you just how
awkward, challenging, and complicated the Christian faith
can be, this chapter just may do it. I know that for many, as
soon as we begin to *talk* about money the squirming, un-
comfortable, look-around-the-room nervousness sets in. But
don't let that happen right now. God isn't stingy, needy, or a

guilt-inducing grouch. He loves his children and wants what's best for us, and generosity is part of that equation.

You've heard it before, and the philosophy isn't going away—money makes the world go around. New York's hip-hop group Wu-Tang Clan says it in their song "C.R.E.A.M.," short for "Cash Rules Everything Around Me." If you don't really grasp your identity as one of Abba's children, you will be tempted to plug what feels like an empty hole in your heart with what money can give you. This can cause incredible pain, sorrow, and regret. The writer of Hebrews told the early church,

> Keep your life free from love of money, and be content with what you have, for he has said, "I will never leave you nor forsake you." So we can confidently say, "The Lord is my helper; I will not fear; what can man do to me?"

Hebrews 13:5–6

Paul told the young pastor Timothy,

> For the love of money is a root of all kinds of evils. It is through this craving that some have wandered away from the faith and pierced themselves with many pangs.

1 Timothy 6:10

Notice that Scripture doesn't condemn having, making, or spending money. Like sex, money is a wonderful thing if stewarded God's way.

God is a generous, loving, and giving God. God gave us his creation, his Word, his Spirit, his people, and the greatest gift he gave us was his Son, the Lord Jesus. When we give, we're reflecting the heart of our Father. The writer of Hebrews encourages us to pursue contentment, which is the opposite of what our world teaches us. We sometimes feel as if we live in the center of Times Square with thousands of ads telling us to buy this bigger, better, faster, more "in" item. But those advertisements on the big screens change every couple of seconds. How are we to keep up? Answer: We don't keep up. In fact, we've dropped out of that race entirely, and we're running toward the heart of God. Notice, too, that our contentment is grounded in the fact that our heavenly Abba will "never leave nor forsake" us! Absolutely nothing can separate us from the love of God (Romans 8) or the presence of God (Psalm 139).

Why is it that we earn money, spend money, and save money all the time, and yet when it comes time to talk about money, we tend to fall off on either side of the horse? For example, some people constantly want to talk about how much money they have and what they are doing with it in an effort to brag and boast in their things. On the other hand, there are those who avoid talking about money at all costs. This could be because they feel they don't have much money or that it is simply bad form to speak of it at all. Like sex, the Bible speaks freely, frequently, and respectfully about money. As you read the Bible, you'll notice that when examined closely, finances is an area of our lives that exposes our heart's truest desires. What we do or don't do with our money has a way of revealing what otherwise would remain concealed from others and even ourselves.

You may have questions like "Does God *actually* expect me to give my money to the church?" "If so, how much?" and "Why does he need my money?" These are all good and legitimate questions that we should ask. But before we dive in to the subject, let me say that when we speak about God's commandments, all of them are couched in the fact that God desires our greatest joy, not our demise. He longs to see his children flourish, not wither up. As with every other discipline that we've talked about, God uses financial giving to conform us to the image of his Son, the Lord Jesus.

God is not out to take something from you; he has something *for* you in the joyous privilege that comes with giving. If you're not totally convinced of this reality, then giving, alongside every other discipline of the faith (like prayer, fasting, serving, etc.) will be one long slog through a swamp, trudging toward a cranky cop on the other side. And that's most certainly *not* the picture of discipleship Jesus painted for us! Jesus envisions our running freely, openly, and joyfully toward our happy and holy Father in heaven, obeying his commandments, and drinking from the fountain of his love for us.

As God addresses money in the lives of his children—those who claim to follow Jesus—you'll sense that he is pressing us toward ultimately putting our money where our mouth is. May we not only proclaim Jesus as Lord in one area, but in every area and avenue of our lives. Like all the chapters of this book, space prohibits a full-blown biblical theology of money and stewardship. So I want to again drive home the *why* behind the *what*, and address some of the relational dynamics at work when it comes to stewarding and giving our money the way God intended. We'll look at Moses, Jesus, and Paul, and we'll see that we simply cannot out give God.

## Moses, Money, and Moving Hearts

Context *always* matters when we study the Scriptures. Let's look at just one passage regarding how the Hebrews were commanded to give during the time of the Exodus. God's people were enslaved under the tyrannical rule of the Pharaohs of Egypt for over four hundred years. They were held captive, abused, and worked endlessly, raising their children in a total nightmare while building the Egyptian empire. They continually called out to Yahweh to rescue, redeem, and deliver them from this horrific oppression. In the famous account of the burning bush, Yahweh says to Moses, "I have indeed seen the misery of my people in Egypt. I have heard them crying out because of their slave drivers, and I am concerned about their suffering" (Exodus 3:7 NIV). God is deeply concerned, and sends Moses to Pharaoh again and again to tell him to release his people. Each time, Pharaoh resists and is met by a plague sent from the hand of God. After the tenth plague, the death of the firstborn, Pharaoh releases the Hebrews, but then changes his mind and pursues them in the desert.

When they come to the Red Sea, God instructs Moses to hold out his staff, and God parts the sea for the people to cross on dry ground! The Egyptian army pursues, but to no avail, as the walls of the sea crash in on them. The Exodus continues as the people wander in the desert. While there, the Lord said to Moses,

> Speak to the people of Israel, that they take for me a contri-
> bution. From every man whose heart moves him you shall

receive the contribution for me. . . . And let them make me
a sanctuary, that I may dwell in their midst.

Exodus 25:1–2, 8

We find God receiving offerings from the people in the
desert because he desires a sanctuary to be constructed in
which he can dwell in their midst. Now stay with me, because this is different from the command that the people give
ten percent (a tithe) of their grain and livestock (Leviticus
27:30–33). God has no needs whatsoever. For example, God
says, "If I were hungry, I would not tell you, for the world
and its fullness are mine" (Psalm 50:12). God could cause a
sanctuary to appear as easily as he spoke creation into existence. So, why the invitation for people to give because their
hearts were moved?

What happened that would cause someone's heart to
move toward worshiping God with their finances? How in
the world could anyone be generous at this place and time?
They are in the desert! Certainly the desert is not a place
for generosity. But remember that the people had just seen
the mighty hand of Yahweh lovingly lead them out from the
captivity of Egypt. After their cries were heard, miracles per-
formed, and deliverance granted, it is not strange to imagine
that many within the camp had hearts overflowing with gratitude. As you'll see throughout Scripture, those who receive
grace give generously. That's just how it works every single
time. Why? Because once truly grasped and experienced,
grace is impossible to keep to oneself. It *has* to be shared! So
there we see grace-motivated generosity in one example in

the Old Testament. Let's look briefly at what Jesus had to say about money.

## Jesus: In God We Trust

What does being a child of God have to do with your money? Everything! Look at this often overlooked verse Luke records. Jesus says,

> But love your enemies, do good to them, and lend to them without expecting to get anything back. Then your reward will be great, and you will be children of the Most High, because he is kind to the ungrateful and wicked.
>
> Luke 6:35

Do you see that the children of God are those who are to love and lend without measure?! To be a bottomless well of love for your enemies and lend to them shows that you're saturated completely in the gospel that teaches, "God so *loved* the world that he *gave* his one and only Son, that whoever believes in him shall not perish but have eternal life" ( John 3:16 NIV). You see, giving always follows loving. That's why Jesus said,

> Do not store up for yourselves treasures on earth. . . . But store up for yourselves treasures in heaven. . . . For where your treasure is, there your heart will be also.
>
> Matthew 6:19–21

Jesus is not out to get the dollars out of our wallets, but to get the idols out of our hearts. He teaches us to pursue the kingdom of God at all costs, to withhold nothing, and to yield literally everything to pursuing him and glorifying God. Once you're a child of the King, you long to see his kingdom come and his will be done. Jesus beautifully summarizes the *joyful obsession* that preoccupies the King's kids:

> The kingdom of heaven is like treasure hidden in a field. When a man found it, he hid it again, and then in his joy went and sold all he had and bought that field.

> Matthew 13:44 NIV

In the parable, the man knows what he's come upon. He's come upon that which is worth more than anything he could ever afford. This treasure is beyond his wildest dreams, and there it is for the taking. He's no fool—he knows just what he's looking at and "in his *joy* went and sold all he had and bought that field."

You see, the pursuit of the kingdom of God is not drudgery! Those who work for God as "employees" find the commandments of God to be boring, taxing, heavy, burdensome work. However, a child of God knows that he's set out on a joy-filled adventure, a never-ending pursuit of what is of infinite value. He's quite literally chasing *glory*. Missionary and martyr Jim Elliot famously said, "He is no fool who gives that which he cannot keep to gain what he cannot lose." When we see the advancement of the gospel, and the enemies of God being reconciled to God and becoming children of God, our hearts are overwhelmed with joy. The giving of our time, our talents, and our money is not always easy or convenient, but it never goes without reward. I strongly encourage you to stay close to Jesus as you seek to be the generous person that God has called you to be.

I've noticed that a generous Christian is often the happiest person in the room. And the flip side of the coin is the same. I've met countless stingy Christians who apparently "had it all" but were the poorest of anyone I've ever known. How is that possible? Because rather than possessing their money, their money possessed them.

As a believer, you should expect to see yourself give more every year. Why is that? Because it is impossible to spend time with Jesus and become less gracious, generous, joyful, understanding, truthful, compassionate, holy, and so on. Those who spend time with Jesus end up becoming like him, and he is the ultimate Giver.

## Paul and the People

If you don't know much about the apostle Paul, read Acts chapters 8 through 28. What you'll find there is that Paul was a very religious, angry man who absolutely despised Christians. He persecuted the church in every way possible, even death. As Paul was on his way to persecute more believers, Jesus appeared to him from heaven, blinded him, rebuked him, and called him to follow after Christ. Paul became one of the leading apostles, planted churches, preached the gospel, made disciples, and poured out his very life for the glory of God and the building up of the church. He wrote much of the New Testament and was masterful in how he went about raising money for the churches in order to carry on their ministries.

In Paul's second letter to the Corinthian church, we find many important insights about raising money. We'll note just a couple here. First, we must see that Paul does not seek to motivate people through fear, guilt, or shame. He knows that those things never build up or achieve the means desired. As in any loving relationship, grace rules, not guilt. So when it comes time to talk about money, he goes not for the wallet, but first to the heart as he points to the cross of Jesus:

> I am not commanding you, but I want to test the sincerity of your love by comparing it with the earnestness of others. For you know the grace of our Lord Jesus Christ, that though he was rich, yet for your sake he became poor, so that you through his poverty might become rich.
>
> 2 Corinthians 8:8–9 NIV

Here Paul is highlighting the incarnation that led to the death of Christ by which we were made rich toward God. In our lowly, needy, bankrupt state, Jesus not only paid our debt, but graciously granted to us his righteousness and gave us the right to be called the children of God. If your church takes Communion weekly, or whenever it does, you'll see who is really giving more. As you take the bread and wine, you'll realize that no matter how big your gift is, nothing compares to the sacrifice Jesus made on our behalf, and that puts our dollars in perspective. We give because he gave.

Second, Paul says, "Each of you should give what you have decided in your heart to give, not reluctantly or under compulsion, for God loves a cheerful giver" (2 Corinthians 9:7 NIV). John Stott wrote of this verse, "There is a sense here of a settled conviction about how much to give; of a decision reached after careful consideration, and always with joy and cheerfulness."[1] God desires for you to sit down and not only consider how to stir one another up to love and good works but also how much you are to be giving. The question of giving is not *if* a believer will give but rather *how much* he or she will give.

I recently had the privilege of worshiping at Redeemer Presbyterian Church on the west side of Manhattan and hearing Dr. Timothy Keller preach a magnificent sermon on giving. He pointed out that most sins are fairly easily identified by others: adultery, murder, stealing, and so forth can be observed. But greed—well, greed is a strange one. You see, you don't have to be rich to be greedy, as Jesus demonstrated so clearly in Luke 21:

> Jesus looked up and saw the rich putting their gifts into the offering box, and he saw a poor widow put in two small copper coins. And he said, "Truly, I tell you, this poor widow has put in more than all of them. For they all contributed out of their abundance, but she out of her poverty put in all she had to live on."
>
> vv. 1–4

Greed is a posture of the heart, and our bank statements reflect this reality. This brings us to Paul's statement about "what you have decided in your heart to give." There's no mention of the tithe, nor has God raised the rent, so to speak. So what are we to do? Paul talks about the condition of our hearts. Keller reminded us of the story in Exodus 16, where manna would appear on the ground as God's way of providing something to eat for the Hebrews who were traveling in the wilderness. Every morning those who were able to go out and gather did so for their own households and for those who were elderly or those who could not gather for themselves. And yet, the Lord had done something unique in his provision. He made the manna so that if one decided to go out and gather more than what was needed it would rot and turn to maggots in the pantry. This was God's way of teaching his people not to hoard up things here on the earth. What does this have to do with our hearts? Everything. You see, if you're greedy and unwilling to share with those in need, then the same principle applies, though this time rottenness doesn't fill your pantry; rottenness will fill your heart.

## What About Tithing?

In the Old Testament, the people were commanded to give a tenth of all they owned to God. In fact, it ended up being closer to 30 percent after all the offerings were accounted for. But what about tithing for New Testament Christians? We do not find an explicit command saying, "This is exactly how much each Christian is expected give." Rather, we find time and time again that Christians gave generously (Acts 2:42–46; 4:32–35). Recall the words Jesus said: "Whoever wants to be my disciple must deny themselves and take up their cross and follow me" (Matthew 16:24 NIV). This was not a metaphorical statement about common inconveniences we face every day like stubbing your toe, having a headache, or being a few minutes late to work. Jesus was on his way to facing a literal cross and prepared his disciples for the same. Thus, to sign up to be a Christian in the first century was to ultimately sign up to lose one's life! If you were to bump into a Christian in the first century and ask them, "Do you tithe?" they may feel quite patronized. The reply would be, "Tithe?! You mean do I give money?! Of course I do! I signed up to lose my life that I may find it!" Jesus lays hold of everything in the life of the believer, including one's income, and he asks his followers to consider how they might steward their resources in order to make the greatest kingdom impact. Trust me, you will never ever regret being generous.

## Poverty Gospel and the Prosperity Gospel

One final word needs to be said about giving, because there are Christians who have a tendency to swing from one end of the pendulum all the way to the other, and at the end base their worth on either how much or how little they have. Some will argue that if you end up totally broke, having given all away, somehow that is the most godly thing one can do. There are others who believe that to measure one's godliness, all you really need to do is look at the house you live in, the cars you drive, and vacations you go on. None of these are accurate reads on righteousness. For our righteousness does not proceed from how much or how little is in the bank. Our righteousness is a gift from Jesus. As you think about money, stewardship, and the kingdom of God, don't make the mistake of thinking that your money defines your worth either in this world or in the eyes of God. You are of infinite value to God because you are made in his image, he has redeemed you through Christ and filled you with the Holy Spirit, and you are his very own child. That is your worth, your identity, your security.

### QUESTIONS TO CONSIDER

1. When talking about giving in the church, what thoughts or emotions come to mind?

2. If you haven't started giving to your church, would you consider starting now? If so, pray it through and determine in your heart to be generous.

3. Do you believe that your generosity and joy are inextricably linked?

# CONCLUSION

## *What Maturity Looks Like*

> Here is the world. Beautiful and terrible things
> will happen. Don't be afraid. I am with you.
> Nothing can ever separate us.
>
> —Frederick Buechner, *Listening to Your Life*

By the time this book is published, I will have been a Christian for just over twenty years. I want to share in this conclusion three things that I have only begun to understand and really apply on an intentional level. These are lessons that I have probably heard here and there along the way for a long time, but only recently has the penny dropped. To be growing as a Christian is to grow in childlikeness, which implies an authentic, joyful trust in the goodness of our Abba. These three lessons I have learned in the hardest season of my life, which should come as no surprise given C. S. Lewis's famous quote from *The Problem of Pain*, where he says, "God whispers to us in our pleasures, speaks in our conscience, but shouts in our pain: it is His megaphone to rouse a deaf world."[1]

## All of Your Wealth Is in Your Relationships

Progressing in gospel-centered maturity means that we begin to find our wealth where we previously saw only rubble. Our flesh is tempted to think that bigger, faster, better, and more proves our wealth. We begin to believe that we are wealthy based on our achievements, accomplishments, titles, possessions, and accolades. Indeed, this is what the world sells every fool on the street, knowing almost no one can resist the sparkly, sugary allurement of sin.

But once we are "in Christ," all of those things are to be understood, accepted, accomplished, and appreciated in light of your new identity. Your truest, deepest wealth comes not from materials or accomplishments, but from relationships. It isn't that all those other things aren't important, they just aren't the *most* important. As you continue to grow and mature in your faith, you start thinking about what and who really matter. Your relationship with Jesus, your spouse, your kids, your friends—they are what matter. If this sounds completely ridiculous, it because you're buying into the lie of the serpent that says, "You are on your own. Make something of yourself. Prove yourself to yourself and everyone else in this world. Use people at all costs and never get too close or too vulnerable with anyone. Protect and save your own soul." But Abba's children don't listen to the Big Bad Wolf anymore.

In this season of life, I'm learning that age plus suffering plus the Holy Spirit's work tend to bring about the kind of childlike joy and contentment that I'm talking about here.

## Jesus Is Gentle

The second thing that I think you'll continually discover throughout your life walking with Jesus is that it's not *if* you fail, but *when* you fail—when you are a mess, frustrated, confused, angry, and full of sin—that Jesus embraces you with unparalleled gentleness. Anyone and everyone either currently confesses Jesus to be Lord and King and Christ or will one day confess him when they see him face-to-face. But those who truly know Jesus in the here and now tend to talk about him in terms of his gentleness. He truly is the great Shepherd, gentle and compassionate toward his harassed and helpless sheep (Matthew 9:36).

As you mature, you'll discover that Jesus doesn't beat the sheep, resent the sheep, or unnecessarily scold the sheep when they screw up. He is out to give life, and life abundantly (John 10:10). In your anger, Jesus remains calm. In your confusion, Jesus brings his presence. In your weeping, Jesus enters, for he is the Man of Sorrows. It is the kindness of God that leads us to repentance (Romans 2:4), and it is the gentleness of Jesus that keeps us coming back to him day in and day out.

## Live Grateful

The last thing I've learned as I make my slow crawl in sanctification, like everyone else, is that gratitude is a sign of biblical maturity. We are by nature selfish, entitled, egotistical, and narcissistic. We tend to think that God and the world owe us something, but the reality is that all God owes us is justice, and the world truly doesn't owe us anything. I'm discovering that I am at my most miserable when I am most ungrateful. For those of us who become children of God through no works of our own, gratitude—a growing in unceasing thanks—ought to permeate our souls. In fact, when we think of ingratitude, could it be the sin that lies beneath all other sins?

Back in the garden of Eden, Adam and Eve were instructed not to touch the one tree, but had everything else available to them: food, Paradise, even the very presence of God. But through conversation with the serpent, deception set in, and they felt entitled to everything in creation, their hearts became ungrateful, and sin entered.

For those who walk with Jesus—knowing his great grace, truth, gentleness, compassion, and faithfulness—gratitude should be the norm. God has given us creation, his Son, the forgiveness of sins, the Holy Spirit, the Word, the church, his kingdom, his covenant, promises, and hope for both now and the age to come! Brennan Manning said, "All is grace."[2] He's right. So for the children of God, there should be only gratitude.

# NOTES

### Introduction: I'm a Christian. Now What?

1. George Wiegel, "Christian Number-Crunching," February 9, 2011, www.firstthings.com/onthesquare/2011/02/christian-number-crunching.

2. Frederick Buechner, *Wishful Thinking: A Seeker's ABC* (San Francisco: Harper & Row, 1973).

3. Quoted in James Davison Hunter, *To Change the World: The Irony, Tragedy, and Possibility of Christianity in the Late Modern World* (New York: Oxford University Press, 2010), 284–285.

### Chapter 1: We Work *From* Not *For* Our Identity

1. Robert Mounce, *Romans: An Exegetical and Theological Exposition of Holy Scripture* (Nashville: Broadman & Holman, 1995), 149.

2. John Owen, *The Mortification of Sin in Believers*, ed. Rev. Terry Kulakowski (Zeeland, MI: Reformed Church Publications, 2015), 17.

3. Mounce, *Romans*, 150.

4. Francis de Sales, *Living the Devout Life* (New York: Sheed and Ward, 1948), 115, quoted in Brennan Manning, *The Signature of Jesus* (Colorado Springs: Multnomah, 1996), 65.

5. *The Book of Common Prayer, Chapel Edition* (New York: Church Publishing, Inc., 1979), 79.

6. Donald Burdick, *Letters of John the Apostle: An In-Depth Commentary* (Chicago: Moody, 1985), 230.

7. Michael Horton, *Christless Christianity* (Grand Rapids, MI: Baker Books, 2008), 102.

## Chapter 2: You Are a Beloved Child of God

1. Kevin DeYoung, *Just Do Something: A Liberating Approach to Finding God's Will* (Chicago: Moody, 2009), 34.

2. John Stott, *The Letters of John*, rev. ed., TNTC (Grand Rapids, MI: Eerdmans, 1988) in D. L. Akin, *1, 2, 3 John* (Nashville: Broadman & Holman, 2001), 133.

3. Akin, *1,2,3 John*, 133.

4. Ronald K. Fung, *New International Commentary on the New Testament: Galatians* (Grand Rapids, MI: Eerdmans, 1988), 185.

5. Martin Luther, *Commentary on Galatians* (Grand Rapids, MI: Revell, 1999), 253.

## Chapter 3: Quit Praying for God to Use You: Real Relationship

1. Graeme Goldsworthy, *Christ-Centered Biblical Theology: Hermeneutical Foundations and Principles* (Downers Grove, IL: InterVarsity, 2012), 75.

## Chapter 4: Don't Fake It With God: Real Prayer

1. Henri Nouwen, *In the Name of Jesus: Reflections on Christian Leadership* (Chestnut Ridge, NY: Crossroad, 1993), 44.

2. A.W. Tozer, *The Knowledge of the Holy: The Attributes of God: Their Meaning in the Christian Life* (San Francisco: HarperCollins, 1961), 1.

3. John Chapman, *Spiritual Letters* (London: Continuum [1935], 2003), 109.

4. Timothy Keller, *Prayer: Experiencing Awe and Intimacy With God* (New York: Penguin, 2014), 228.

5. Paul House, "Sin in the Law," in Christopher W. Morgan and Robert A. Peterson, eds., *Fallen: A Theology of Sin* (Wheaton, IL: Crossway, 2013), 43.

6. D.A. Carson, *Jesus' Sermon on the Mount and His Confrontation with the World: An Exposition of Matthew 5–10* (Grand Rapids, MI: Baker Books, 1987), 76.

7. N.T. Wright, *Surprised by Hope: Rethinking Heaven, the Resurrection, and the Mission of the Church* (San Francisco: HarperOne, 2008), 293.

8. Father Thomas Keating, quoted in Mark Nepo, *The Book of Awakening: Having the Life You Want by Being Present to the Life You Have* (San Francisco: Conari Press, 2000), 268.

9. Brennan Manning, *The Ragamuffin Gospel: Good News for the Bedraggled, Beat-Up, and Burnt-Out* (Colorado Springs: Multnomah, 2005), 155.

10. *The Apostle* (Universal, 1997), written and directed by Robert Duvall. Quoted in Craig Brian Larson and Andrew Zahn, *Movie-Based Illustrations for Preaching and Teaching* (Grand Rapids, MI: Zondervan, 2003), 212–213.

## Chapter 5: Real Obedience

1. Manning, *The Ragamuffin Gospel*, 112.

2. Martin Brecht, *Martin Luther: His Road to Reformation, 1483–1521*, trans. James L. Schaff (Minneapolis: Fortress Press, 1985), 192.

3. Phillip Cary, *Jonah: Brazos Theological Commentary on the Bible* (Grand Rapids, MI: Brazos, 2008), 17.

4. Will Durant, *The Story of Civilization: Part 1, Our Oriental Heritage* (New York: Simon & Schuster, 1954), 269.

5. Thomas à Kempis, *The Imitation of Christ*, rewritten and updated by Harold J. Chadwick (Alachua, FL: Bridge-Logos, 1999), 24.

6. Lucius Annaeus Seneca, *Anger, Mercy, Revenge*, trans. Robert A. Kaster and Martha C. Nussbaum (Chicago: The University of Chicago Press, 2010), 54.

## Chapter 6: Baptism: Cleansed

1. J.I. Packer, *Concise Theology: A Guide to Historic Christian Beliefs* (Carol Stream, IL: Tyndale, 1993), 212.

2. Steven Gertz, "What is the pre-Christian history of the baptismal ceremony?" *Christianity Today*, August 8, 2008, www.christianitytoday.com/ch/asktheexpert/mar14.html.

3. "Baptism," in Leland Ryken, James C. Wilhoit, and Tremper Longman III, gen. eds., *Dictionary of Biblical Imagery* (Downers Grove, IL: InterVarsity, 1998), 73.

4. Justo L. González, *The Story of Christianity: The Early Church to the Dawn of the Reformation*, vol. 1 (San Francisco: Harper & Row, 1984), 96.

5. L. Morris, *The Gospel According to Matthew* (Grand Rapids, MI; Leicester, England: Eerdmans; InterVarsity Press, 1992), 748.

6. "Baptism," in Ryken, Wilhoit, and Longman III, gen. eds., *Dictionary of Biblical Imagery*, 73.

7. D.G. Peterson, *The Acts of the Apostles* (Grand Rapids, MI; Nottingham, England: Eerdmans, 2009), 603.

8. Ibid.

9. Sofia Cavalletti, *Living Liturgy: Elementary Reflections* (Chicago: Archdiocese of Chicago Liturgy Training Publications, 1998), 57–58.

## Chapter 7: Church Membership

1. Jonathan Leeman, *Church Membership: How the World Knows Who Represents Jesus* (Wheaton, IL: Crossway, 2012), 64.

2. In interest of space, I did not go into discussion of the role of deacons or any other office in the church.

3. Steve Timmis and Tim Chester, *Total Church: A Radical Reshaping around Gospel and Community* (Wheaton, IL: Crossway, 2008), 88.

## Chapter 8: Life in the Church Community

1. See Justin Holcomb, *Know the Creeds and Councils* (Grand Rapids, MI: Zondervan, 2014).

## Chapter 9: What About My Money?

1. John Stott, *The Living Church: Convictions of a Lifelong Pastor* (Downers Grove, IL: InterVarsity, 2007), 132.

## Conclusion: What Maturity Looks Like

1. C.S. Lewis, *The Problem of Pain* (New York: HarperCollins, 2001), 92.
2. Brennan Manning, *All Is Grace: A Ragamuffin Memoir* (Colorado Springs: David C. Cook, 2011), 27.

# Christianese Glossary

This is an attempt at providing you with a glossary of terms Christians use. *Christianese* is in and of itself an *insider* term. Basically, it refers to language that only surfaces in Christian circles and often includes the use of metaphors that only make sense after being in the church for a while. We thought it would be helpful to provide you with a number of examples—some serious and some funny. Enjoy!

**Backslidden**—The term refers to claiming to be a Christian, but not living like it. Or, of returning to a state of practicing sin, but not repenting of it.

**Bless your heart**—This is an expression that thrives in the southeastern U.S. It's patronizing in most cases. Example: "Hey, Mom, I tried to open this can of beans with a hammer." "Oh really?" replies Mom. "Well, bless your heart." Translation: "Nice try, stupid."

**Born again**—Refers to the experience of being regenerated, transformed by God in response to a repentant prayer of faith to be forgiven and become a new creation in Christ (John 3; 2 Corinthians 5:17).

**Closed doors.** Or, **"When God closes one door he opens another"** or **"When God closes a door he opens a window."**—These basically mean that when one thing doesn't work out, something else will.

**Dating Jesus**—You might hear a single person say this. Probably needs no definition.

**Disciplined**—The Bible speaks about the Lord disciplining those he loves (Hebrews 12:5–7). Christians will sometimes use it to say, "Things just aren't going my way."

**Doing life together**—This is how some Christians speak about their friends and themselves when they are involved together in small discipleship groups.

**Echo**—The equivalent of a retweet in prayer. Example: "Lord, I just want to echo what Jed prayed a moment ago."

**Feeling led.** Or, **"I feel led to do that"** or **"I don't feel led to do that"**— These essentially mean the person either wants to do something or doesn't want to do it, and is involving the Lord in the decision.

**Fellowshipping**—Also known as "hanging out with friends"—in the Lord, of course.

**Fire**—In general, Christians use fire as a way of speaking of devotion, power, excitement, worship, progress. Some examples are (1) When speaking of someone who is passionate about evangelism: "He's on fire for the Lord." (2) In prayer: "Jesus, set your church on fire!"

**Hedge of protection.** As in, **"Put a hedge of protection around them."**— This phrase is used in prayer by Christians, asking the Lord to circle someone with an impenetrable barrier, whether invisible or with visible angels. Sometimes misunderstood by those who think Satan must hate shrubbery.

**In this place**—A phrase in prayer referring to the actual place or situation being addressed. Example: "Lord, meet with us *in this place*."

**Let go and let God**—An imperative that means to cease being anxious about a situation, or hanging on to someone or something, and trust the sovereignty of God to work and intervene.

**Love on.** As in, **"I just want to love on you."**—A phrase that means to show someone you care. (But it sure doesn't sound right.)

**Married in our hearts**—This phrase is sometimes used by a couple who has entered into a serious relationship—whether by living together or otherwise having sex outside of marriage. The Bible teaches that an intimate sexual relationship is reserved only for marriage. So this expression is thrown out as a way of avoiding conviction?

**Mmmmhmmmmmmm**—This is *not* speaking in tongues. It's what you'll sometimes hear when someone agrees with the preacher but doesn't necessarily want to say "Amen."

**Mysterious ways.** As in, **"The Lord works in mysterious ways."**—This is what Christians say when something unexplainable happens and they attribute it to the working of God.

**More than you can handle.** As in, **"God won't give you more than you can handle."**—This is a statement Christians use for someone who is going through difficult times. The aim is to point out that the situation could be worse. It is taken from Paul's words to the Corinthians: "No temptation has overtaken you that is not common to man. God is faithful, and he will not let you be tempted beyond your ability, but with the temptation he will also provide the way of escape, that you may be able to endure it" (1 Corinthians 10:13).

**Nourishment**—This is referenced in prayers around the table, regardless of what is served. As in, "Lord, bless this Big Mac to the nourishment of my body."

**O Lord, Father God**—While addressing the Lord in prayer, this is often a space filler when one runs out of things to say.

**Pour into.** As in, **"Can we just pour into each other?"**—This is a request Christians use when they want to build one another up. However, like "love on," it sounds somewhat bizarre.

**Prayer warrior**—Referring to someone who prays a whole lot. Also meaning someone who has a gift of intercession for the lost.

**Quiet time**—This term speaks of spending a consistent, regular time alone with God, reading the Bible and in prayer.

**Receive.** As in, **"I receive that."**—This is used when someone agrees with something spiritual someone has said. Closely related: **"I don't receive that."**—Used when someone refuses to listen to or heed whatever is being said.

**Seasons**—Just like the calendar seasons of the year, Christians will often use this term to define how they're doing, what they're focusing on, or going through, with the understanding that life won't always hold the current circumstance. Example: "In this season, I feel like the Lord is really teaching me to be generous."

**Self-deprecating talk/prayers**—Occasionally, you'll hear someone in prayer or in conversation putting themselves down, often in an attempt to sound more pious than thou. Example: "Lord, you know what a wretched piece of garbage I am."

**Traveling mercies**—This is referred to by Christians praying for one another before embarking on a trip (usually a mission trip). Example: "Lord, we pray for traveling mercies for our youth pastor and these high schoolers as they make their way to Timbuktu."

**Unspoken**—These are prayer requests that are too private or embarrassing to voice to a group, thus they remain "unspoken."

**Vestibule/Narthex**—The place where one shakes the pastor's hand on the way out. Also known as the "lobby."

**Washed in the blood**—This refers to being cleansed in the blood of Christ, who died for the sins of the whole world.

**Alex Early** is the author of *The Reckless Love of God* and serves Redemption Church in Seattle, Washington, where he focuses on preaching and theology. He has completed two master's degrees (MDiv, New Orleans Baptist Theological Seminary and MA in Aspects of Biblical Interpretation, London School of Theology) and is a current doctoral candidate (Doctor of Intercultural Studies, Western Seminary). Alex has been heavily involved in training church leaders both in the U.S. and abroad. He is a sought-after speaker and lives with his wife, Jana, and their two children in Seattle. Find out more at Alxegesis.com.

# More From
# Alex Early

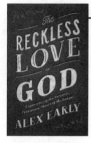

In *The Reckless Love of God*, pastor and church planter Alex Early pulls you in close to ask if you've ever really considered what it means to say "Jesus loves me." God's love for us is real—he feels, knows, and even suffers on our behalf. Nothing will change your life, your goals, and your relationships faster than being captivated by this reality. Whether you grew up as a Christian and have forgotten this essential truth or you're hearing it for the first time, you need to be reminded—and assured—of the simple, amazing, mind-blowing fact that God loves us.

*The Reckless Love of God*